How to Read ... ies

How to Read Bible Stories

An introduction to narrative criticism

Daniel Marguerat and Yvan Bourquin

with the collaboration of Marcel Durrer

Illustrations by Florence Clerc

SCM PRESS

Translated by John Bowden from the French *Pour lire les récits bibliques*, published 1998 by Les Éditions du Cerf, Paris.

0 334 02778 0

This edition first published 1999 by
SCM Press
9–17 St Albans Place London N1 0NX

SCM Press is a division of SCM-Canterbury Press Ltd

Typeset by Rowland Phototypesetting Ltd,
Bury St Edmunds, Suffolk
Printed in Great Britain by
Redwood Books, Trowbridge, Wiltshire

Contents

Contents

Contents

Preface

Story-telling is as old as the world. Human beings, men and women, have always told stories and told about themselves. Their intentions have been countless: to teach, to communicate, to console, to bear witness, to distract... Narrative after narrative, and each time the magic of the story is reborn.

Believers, too, have told stories since the dawn of time. Israel lived by telling and retelling the story begun between God and his people. And among the first Christians, once the splendour of Pentecost was over, tongues were untied. Since then the biblical stories have been handed down, from generation to generation, feeding the faith and setting the imagination on fire. The Bible is one of the most fabulous treasuries of stories (history) ever given to humankind.

Now there are two types of reader (one can be both at once). The first reader is carried away by the narrative. The second wants to know how to set about understanding the author in order to be carried away by the narrative. For stories are not told just anyhow. The biblical narratives, fashioned over a long period in an oral context and patiently edited by pious authors, follow subtle rules of composition. How are they constructed? What effects did the narrators want to produce? How do they guide the attention of the reader? What signals, given in the text, pilot the reader in understanding the story? A recent method, narrative criticism, sets out to illuminate the workings of biblical narration. But there should be no misunderstanding about what is involved: to bring out the hidden architecture of the texts is to question their significance in a new way.

This book is meant to enable readers to become familiar with the approach and procedures of narrative criticism. It has been planned as a manual: it describes and applies the tools of this approach in such a way that readers can go on to use them by themselves. To achieve the greatest possible clarity, the material will be presented in a system which is immediately obvious. No concept will be introduced without being described and defined. The boxes develop specific points; readers in a hurry can skip them. The test questions ('Check your knowledge') offer readers an opportunity to evaluate how much they have taken in: the answers appear at the end of the book. With the exception of the first two introductory chapters, the chapters can be read in any order; a system of internal references (e.g. >3.2), two indexes and a glossary at the end of the book make it possible for readers to refer back to definitions and find their way around the book.

Florence Clerc and Marcel Durrer have done wonders in improving the readability of the book, the former by her drawings and the latter by his help with the test questions and his competence in the Old Testament. We also want to thank friends who have helped us by making suggestions after reading the text: Diane Barraud, Bernard Bolay, Pierre-Yves Brandt, Claude Jaques, Sophie Reymond and Anne-Laure Zwilling. Emmanuelle Steffek has been a tremendous help in checking the text at various stages and compiling the indexes.

And now we make our way through the biblical narrative. It has been produced over centuries, but the work of the story-tellers and their secrets are waiting to be unveiled...

Daniel Marguerat and Yvan Bourquin

Rembrandt (1606–1669), *The Reader*, 1634, etching.
Fondation W. Cuendet and Atelier de St-Prex, Musée Jenisch, Vevey. Photo Studio É. Curchod.

1

Entering the world
of the narrative

One day Jesus used an attractive image, that of the scribe who, like an owner, 'takes from his treasure things new and old' (Matt.13.52). One could apply this to narrative criticism: this type of reading explores with new tools an art which is as old as the world, the art of story-telling.

The question of the composition of the biblical narratives is not intrinsically new. St Augustine, who was a perceptive reader, asked himself why the Bible sometimes lost itself in *superfluitates*, in apparently superfluous details of geography, clothing or perfume. Could it be that the divine Inspirer of the scriptures was wasting his time with worldly preoccupations? Clearly not. If the story dwells on these details, says Augustine, it is to warn us to read them in a figurative sense, as a symbol or an allegory. The fundamental intuition of narrative criticism was already there: every narrative is composed with a view to having an effect on the reader: it is a matter of discovering in the text signals which mark out and orientate the course of reading.

In the tools which it provides and which this book will present one after another, narrative criticism still mixes the old and the new. More than one concept goes back to the most ancient specialist in narrative, a fourth-century BC Greek philosopher, Aristotle. His treatise on *Poetics* lays theoretical foundations to which we shall constantly be return-

ing. Here we see studied for the first time the phenomenon of *narrativity*. Narrativity is the totality of characteristics which make a text a narrative, different from a discourse or a description. The narrative features by which one identifies a narrative (let us say for the moment it is telling a story) differ from the discursive features by which one identifies a speech (which addresses its audience directly).

So narrative criticism is a method of reading the text which explores and analyses how narrativity is made concrete in a particular text. To take up Augustine's question again, narrative criticism will ask itself what function is assumed by the 'details' of the text, in what order they appear, what information they give to the reader, and so on.

The scientific study of narrativity has a name, *narratology*; this science is recent, even if sometimes it reformulates and refines ancient concepts. The theoreticians of narratology (both European and American) published their works from the 1960s and 1970s on; its application to biblical narrativity came a decade later.

Let's begin by noting the project of narrative criticism, comparing it to other kinds of reading applied to the biblical narrative today (1.1). We shall do this by demonstrating rapidly how, by whom and from what narrative criticism arose (1.2). Then we shall spend some time on the two poles of narrative communication, looking at the relationship between narrator and narratee (1.3) and the redefinition of the author and the reader (1.4). Finally we shall spell out precisely what is understood by 'narrative' (1.5).

1.1 What does narrative criticism look for?

Every reading defines itself by the questions that it addresses to the text. It is naïve to think that there is one reading which is better than all the rest. Let's say, rather, that there is a plurality of readings, each differing in what it is looking for in the text: the reading can be guided by a historical, a psychoanalytical, a structural, a symbolic interest, etc. Depending on their questions, readers will opt for one type of analysis rather than another.

The appearance of a new type of reading always indicates that a shift of approach is offered. This new questioning will be matched by a new approach, using new operative concepts. By comparison with existing readings, narrative analysis also shifts the questioning: it has had to equip itself with adequate tools to explore its questions. But what shift is this?

Jakobson's scheme

We need to take a theoretical detour to grasp the issue. We shall borrow this schematic presentation of verbal communication from the linguist Roman Jakobson in his *Essais de linguistique générale* (214, 220):

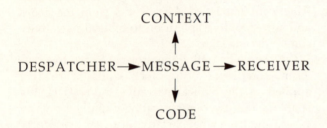

Every verbal communication, says Jakobson, consists in sending a *message* from a *despatcher* to a *receiver*. Now every message has two aspects, the *context* and the *code*. If the message is 'Your pear is green', the context is the world of representation to which it relates: in order to grasp the message the receiver must know what an pear is and what colour green is. To study the reality to which the text refers is to be interested in its referential function. But the message also relates to a linguistic code: the receiver must know how to differentiate the phoneme <pear> from the phoneme <bear> or< tear>. In short, if it is to be received adequately, every message needs an agreement between the recipient and the despatcher on the reality represented and the linguistic code used.

To study the context is to analyse the *referential* function of the message (the reality to which it refers). To be interested in the code is to take into consideration the *metalinguistic* function of the message (to identify the code common to the despatcher and the receiver). Transposed to the reading of a text, Jakobson's scheme can be reformulated as follows: the author transmits to the reader a literary work which on the one hand relates to the world represented (the information) and on the other articulates and makes a network of the verbal signs (the language).

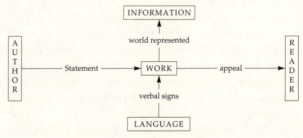

Robert M. Fowler, who has proposed this reformulation of Jakobson's scheme in *Let the Reader Understand* (54–5), has noted that the textual communication necessarily links two axes. The vertical

4

axis is the mimetic axis or the axis of representation: it encompasses the representation of the world which the literary work gives on the basis of the linguistic code used. The horizontal axis is the rhetorical axis or the axis of communication: it characterizes the relationship which is formed between author and reader by the intervention of the literary work.

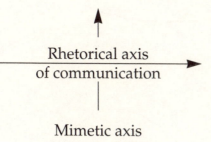

Rhetorical axis
of communication

Mimetic axis
of representation

Jakobson's scheme is very useful, since it makes it possible to locate and differentiate three major types in reading the Bible.

Three readings

If we look at Francophone exegesis, for the most part two types of analysis are used in reading the Bible: historical criticism and structural analysis (or semiotics). The third type presented will be narrative criticism.

What does historical criticism look for? It is interested in the historical event related by the text and the conditions in which the text has been written. Generally speaking, its interest is fixed on the (historical) world *behind* the text. Faced with the little narrative of the healing of Simon's mother-in-law (Mark 1.29-31), historical criticism asks: What really happened? How did this tradition come down to the evangelist Mark? How did this author interpret it for the community to which he addresses his Gospel, around the 60s of our era? The aim here is to reconstruct on the one hand the reality to which the narrative relates and on the other the intention of the author who composes it.

What does structural or semiotic analysis look for? This type of reading gravitates around the south pole of the axis of representation, whereas historical criticism is located to the north. Structural analysis is not at all interested in the world that is represented but in the functioning of language. It follows a principle which is called the postulate of immanence: nothing outside the text, nothing but the text and the whole text (everything is taken account of in the text; no information is taken from outside the text). Its question is: how does the text go about producing meaning? The text is read as a system of signs, and it is necessary to understand how they are organized into a network. The narrative in Mark 1.29-31 will be the occasion to examine the use of space, the transition made by the woman from lying down to getting up, the opposition between Jesus who approaches and the fever which departs. The world to be explored does not lie behind the text; it is the *world of the text* that has to be gone through.

Where is narrative criticism to be located? Not on the axis of representation but on the axis of communication. Its question is: How does the author communicate his message to the reader? By what strategy does the author organize the decipherment of meaning by the reader? The study here relates to the structuring which allows the message to have the effect sought by the despatcher. Again in the case of the healing of Simon's mother-in-law, here attention is paid to the order in which the characters enter the story (why does Jesus appear last?), to the prominent role of the disciples (they make Jesus act) and to the effect of the healing (the woman serves them).

HISTORICAL CRITICISM

NARRATIVE CRITICISM

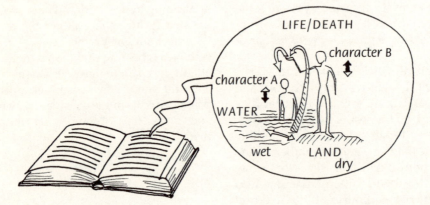

SEMIOTIC (OR STRUCTURAL) ANALYSIS

Author – message – reader

We could put it in yet a different way. The axis of communication aligns the three poles without which no transmission is possible: the author (despatcher), the message, the reader (receiver). The historical-critical reading is orientated on the pole of the *author*; it investigates what traditions he has gathered and how he has transmitted and interpreted them. The semiotic reading addresses the *text* and listens to its codes of communication; it is interested in the message. Narrative criticism is primarily orientated neither on the author nor on the message, but on the *reader*: it has in view the effect of the narrative on the readers and the way in which the text makes them cooperate in deciphering the meaning.

But we should be aware of hardening the typology which has just been sketched out. The historical reading is not uninterested in the receiver, and narrative criticism does not skip the question of the author; its fixation on the reader indicates the pole from which all its questioning is organized. At the opposite end from the generative approach of the historical reading (which fixes the rules by which a writing is produced independently of the effects which it prompts) are the so-called *pragmatic* readings, which include narrative criticism, rhetorical criticism, reader-response criticism and deconstructionism. Readings which are interested in investigating the effect of the text on the reader are called *pragmatic*. They have adequate equipment for discovering the pragmatic indications in the text, namely the instructions for interpretation, suggesting to the reader how the text should be received. Rhetorical criticism has the mandate when it comes to argumentative texts, i.e. discourses (its main area in the New Testament is the Pauline correspondence).

The two pragmatic readings, narrative criticism and rhetorical criticism, are twin sisters in their questioning: both are of recent creation, and their origin is more American than European.

No exclusiveness

Once again, every reading is valid for its own type of questioning. It is also a matter of being attentive to the questions that the text raises or supports. The fundamentally historical character of the biblical texts certainly calls for a reading which is interested in history, but not exclusively. Here we shall show how fruitful an analysis can be which it is attached to the narrative dimension; this is no substitute for historical-critical study but it allows sense to emerge which escape historical criticism.

However, we must not conceal the distance which separates historical criticism from the two others. Historical criticism offers an interpretation centred on history (that of the text and that which the text relates); semiotics and narrative criticism make common cause in developing an interpretation focussed on the text. To emphasize this: contrary to the historical reading, narrative criticism and semiotics refuse to base their approach on a reconstruction on the social and cultural environment of the text (when, where and how it was written). But unlike semiotics, narrative criticism envisages the text as a process of communication between author and reader: semiotics cuts the link between author and text and refuses to speak of an intention of the author on the meaning. We shall spell out later (>1.4) what we understand here by author and reader.

1.2 The history of a birth

When was narrative criticism born? To meet what needs? What was the origin of this shift in reading to which its questions bear witness?

A bit of history. In 1981, a book by Robert Alter was published in New York which was to prove to have a powerful influence on biblical exegesis: *The Art of Biblical Narrative*. As we have seen, Alter was not the first to ask how the Bible tells stories: but for the first time a study systematically reviewed the characteristics of biblical narration. The field in which Robert Alter established himself was the Hebrew Bible. The questions which guided his research are not usual in exegesis: How does the narrator compose the scenes? What is the function of dialogue in narrative? What is the purpose of the repetitions in a story? What knowledge is communicated to the reader and what is concealed? How does the narrator introduce the characters and how does he make them develop? The most astonishing thing is that the authors on which Alter based himself to solve these questions were not the approved exegetes of the Old Testament but Homer and Rabelais, Gustave Flaubert, Ibn Ezra and Charles Dickens.

The research of Robert Alter is representative of a new type of reading formed in the United States at the end of the 1970s, narrative criticism. His book is the first striking application of narrative criticism to the sphere of biblical literature. Now Alter is not a theologian. He is a literary critic interested in the Bible. In his reading he makes use of his knowledge of literature and the great authors, but equally of his familiarity with the Jewish traditions. We need to note a first indication here: the two sources the meeting of which gave birth to narrative criticism are on the one hand the burst of interest in narrativity in literary criticism and on the other the narrative sensitivity shown by the Jewish tradition of the Midrash.

The meeting of two worlds

The same characteristics stamp the publication, a year later, of the work of David Rhoads and Donald Michie, *Mark as Story*. This work is the first study to take account of the narrative of a biblical book as a whole. To put it another way, this book is the first to consider a biblical author exclusively as a writer, and to set out to describe his procedures in writing.

This original enterprise is based on an experience: the request made by Rhoads to his colleague Michie, a professor of English literature, to join his course on the Bible to get the students to read the Gospel of Mark as one reads a novel. The methodological apparatus on which these two researchers rely is shaped by a collection of works which one could bring together under the heading of 'new literary criticism'. Here we find the names of Seymour Chatman (1978) and Wayne Booth (1961) for rhetoric and fiction; Paul Ricoeur (1983–1985) and Gérard Genette (1972) for the study of narrativity; Boris Uspensky (1973) for textual poetics; and Wolfgang Iser (1972) for the notion of the reader. The term narrative criticism comes from David Rhoads.

We should note a second indication: narrative criticism did not come out of a single brain. This concept was constructed in the United States with the help of theoretical work carried out by French, German and American scholars on narrativity, and it bears witness to a fruitful encounter between the

---

DEFINITIONS

Narratology: a science the object of which is the study of narrativity (textual or artistic).

Narrativity: the totality of characteristics by which a text (or a work) is recognizable as a narrative (inventory of characteristics: > 1.5).

Pragmatic reading: a method of reading which questions the text in terms of the effects that it has on the reader: it discovers in it the pragmatic indi-

cations which are the instructions suggesting to the reader the way in which the text is to be received. Narrative criticism relates to the narrative, rhetorical criticism covers the field of discourse.

Narrative criticism: a reading of a pragmatic type which studies the effects of the meanings brought out by the arrangement of the narrative: it presupposes that this arrangement implements a narrative strategy directed at the reader.

THE TRANSITION FROM WHY TO HOW

Historical criticism, which has had a monopoly of the scientific study of the Bible since the eighteenth century, inherited a Romantic conception of literature (Schleiermacher, Dilthey); its axiom was that only the genesis of texts gives access to the intention of their authors. So the analysis is historical, imitating the natural sciences which explain phenomena and establish their causes. The cardinal question is 'why?' Why has the text been conceived in this way, by what author, in what sphere of production, and for what historical audience?

The new literary criticism, a vast current of which both semiotics (or structural analysis) and narrative criticism are heirs, breaks with this questioning. It is part of a radical change of paradigm in literary studies, heralded by H.R.Jauss in 1969, which swings interest from the pole of the author to the pole of the reader. The ambition is to free the text from any tyranny which might make it depend on its author, its history or the milieu in which it was produced. The affinity between semiotics and narrative criticism relates to three common postulates (we shall spell out in a moment what separates them).

1. The text is not read as a document relating to a historical world outside it; it is not received as a document but as a monument which has a value of its own, as an autonomous work, unfolding a narrative world the coherence of which has to be found.

2. The text is read in its final form, and the understanding of its function is not guided by its genealogy. The question slips from 'why?' to 'how?': How does the narrative make sense? How and in what stages has it been constructed?

3. It is impossible to get at the person of the historical author or the original audience for the writing. In short, the work must be read independently of any hypothesis about the context of the original communication of the writing.

Semiotics and narrative criticism thus share a postulate of autonomy which is accorded to the work to make sense (autonomy from the historical milieu which produced it: I do not need to know the evangelist John to read and understand his Gospel). Where is the break between these two types of reading? It takes place at two points.

First, the story is received in narratology as a textual object communicated by the despatcher to the receiver. It is postulated that through the text the despatcher wants to act on the receiver, and the narratologists are interested in discovering the narrative strategy deployed in the story with a view to acting on the receiver. By contrast, semiotics has a horror of speaking of narrative strategy; its view is that to accept this amounts to taking meaning to be a product ready to be consumed by the reader. Conversely, narratology thinks that reading consists in respecting the constraints of the signifiers and that the constraints used by the author conceal a strategy of narrative communication.

Secondly, while narratology abdicates before the possibility of reconstructing the identity of the author and the historical recipients of the writing (who wrote the book of Jonah and with what intention), it does not give up reconstructing their narrative identity. Here we touch on an important point which distinguishes semiotics from narrative criticism. The narratologists are aware that the relation established between an author and his work is complex. As a historical figure, Zola exists independently of his novels. Nevertheless, each of his stories gives an image of himself (which can be different from the historical character). Similarly, the text gives us access to the image that the narrator makes (or wants to give) of his audience, and not their real identity. Later in the chapter we shall see how this narrative image of the author and the reader can be identified (<1.3 and 1.4).

Further reading

M. A. Powell, *What is Narrative Criticism?*, Minneapolis: Fortress Press 1990, 1–21 (historical criticism and literary criticism: differences in method).

world of literature and the world of exegesis. Its equipment for reading systematizes the results of these works. The totality is composite, since in it we find side by side references to classical drama (the notion of character) and legacies from semiotics (the plot or narrative programme), allied to new factors (the concept of the author and the reader, temporality, narrative rhetoric).

It goes without saying that like any scientific discovery, the birth of a new type of reading can be explained by the cultural environment from which it arises. To be brief, let us say that following a loss of credibility on the part of historical research, it emanates from a shift in the order of knowledge from 'why' to 'how'.

1.3 Narrator and narratee

Jakobson's scheme has shown us the function performed, at the two poles of communication, by the transmitter of the message (despatcher) and the one who receives it (receiver). In narrative criticism the one who tells the story is called the narrator and the one who comes to know it through the reading is called the narratee. The narrator is (to take an attractive image used by Gérard Genette) the 'voice' which tells the story and guides the reader in the narrative.

The narrator can be explicitly present in the story that he tells ('This morning I met a man who. . .'); in the case of autobiography the narrator even becomes the main character of the story that he tells. He can also be absent from the narrative, and that is the case with most novels. However, even if he does not figure explicitly (through an 'I') in the story, the narrator remains present in the background; as the director of the story he occupies the place of the producer at the theatre or the film director.

In biblical narration it is rare for the narrator to put himself forward. Traditionally the biblical narrator effaces himself behind the story that he tells: he remains the servant who withdraws behind the events that he puts forward. However, narrative

criticism gives us occasion to note that this explicit effacement of the narrator does not prevent him from being very much present through the narrative strategy which he deploys.

However, there are some rare exceptions to this absence of the narrator from the story. Luke the evangelist makes himself known by a preface in which both narrator and narratee are named: 'Inasmuch as many have undertaken to compile a narrative of the events which have been accomplished among us. . . it seemed good to me also, having followed all things closely for some time past, to write an orderly account for you, most excellent Theophilus. . .' (Luke 1.1–3, cf. Acts 1.1). This is an exception. Under the cover of a dedication, the narrator includes in the text itself the recipient (concrete? ideal?) of his story: suddenly the character of Theophilus becomes the position for the reader to take, the next verse indicating the aim of the reading: '. . .that you may know the truth concerning the things of which you have been informed' (Luke 1.4).

Here or there the narrator indicates himself obliquely (John 19.35; 21.24) or inserts into his text a 'we' which can include the narratee (Luke 1.3; John 1.14–16). The narrator may even include himself in a group which features in the story that he tells: this is the case in the famous 'we' sequences in the book of Acts (16.10–17; 20.5–15; 21.1–18; 27.1–28.16). We shall be pursuing these analyses later (> 2.6).

An omniscient and trustworthy narrator

The moment the reader becomes involved in the reading or, if you like, the moment the reader adopts the position of narratee, by implication he enters into a contract with the narrator. Narrator and narratee are linked in the process of reading. What makes up this link?

Let's take the book of Job as an example. The first sentence is: 'There was a man in the land of Uz whose name was Job, and that man was blameless and upright, one who feared God and turned away from evil' (Job 1.1). What an incredible statement!

Can one really claim of anyone, without reservation or exception, that he fears God and turns away from evil? Now this initial statement plays an important role in the drama of the book of Job: Job's protest against the misfortune that he undergoes is based on the integrity of his life. The story continues with a dialogue at the heavenly court between God and the Satan (Job 1.6–12). In the real world we would ask about both the integrity of Job and the realism of this heavenly audience. In the world of the narrative the narratee accepts being led by the narrator – or he closes the book.

So an implied contract is made between the narrator and the narratee at the beginning of the story. This contract recognizes the omniscience and the trustworthiness of the narrator. Let's spell this out.

The narrator is recognized as omniscient. He can relate to us the audience in the heavenly court (Job 1). He can also describe for us a private scene at which no one is supposed to be present: the agony of Jesus in Gethsemane (Mark 14.32–42). He can tells us what is happening in two places at the same time: within the palace of Annas and in the court-yard of the palace at the time of Peter's denial (John 18.12–27). He can make us share in events which no other person has witnessed: the inner thoughts of the scribes (Mark 3.2); Joseph's dream (Matt.2.19–20); the feelings of Jesus (Mark 5.30); the creation of the world (Gen.1–2). In short, not only is the narrator in a position to know everything, but he does not even have to give account of the origin of his knowledge.

Furthermore the reader has trust in the narrator. He recognizes that the narrator is trustworthy. This is uniformly the case in biblical narration: the reader sticks to the narrator's story, to his system of values. And when the narrator of the books of Kings distinguishes between the kings who please God and those whose actions do not please God, the reader acquiesces. That having been said, the trustworthiness of the narrator is not a narrative dogma: narratives can play on the untrustworthiness of a narrator (that is the case in a detective story, in which the narrator hides important clues from the reader).

The narrative of II Samuel 14 presents us with an untrustworthy narrator, but that happens within the story that is being told. 'So he (Joab) sent to Tekoa, and fetched from there a wise woman, and said to her, "Pretend to be a mourner, and put on mourning garments; do not anoint yourself with oil, but behave like a woman who has been mourning many days for the dead; and go to the king and speak thus to him. . ."' (II Sam.14.2–3).

The collaboration of the reader

These first remarks on the relationship between the narrator and the narratee open up a vast area for us to reflect on, which can be summed up under the following question: what feeds the collaboration between narrator and narratee? For the narrator certainly needs the narratee to decipher the narrative. He will guide the narratee and help him in this operation. He will transmit signals to make him understand. He will give him the information that he wants when he wants it.

Alongside the role of the narrator (which is evident in the control of the story), the role attributed to the reader is set down in the text, but under the surface. In this connection some narratologists, like Paul Ricoeur, speak of an interaction between text and reader. Others, like Umberto Eco, speak of the co-operation of the reader (who has the initiative in interpretation and actualization). Yet others emphasize the experience of reading, in the course of which narrator and narratee are put in communication with the aid of the text (this position is defended by the so-called school of 'reader-response criticism'). We shall be exploring this field of interaction in Chapter 9.

1.4 The narrative authorities

Who are we talking about when we speak of the author and the reader? We have already indicated that the narrator is not to be confused with the author, but now this approach must be refined. For narrative criticism does quite original work on this point.

Author and real reader

What happens when someone composes a narrative? Mr X (let us say Anthony Trollope) produces a text for a circle of readers (the future readers of his novel). We shall call Anthony Trollope the real author and the circle of readers for whom he intends his work the real readers. Similarly, one day there was an evangelist (to whom by convention we give the name Matthew) who composed a Gospel intended to be read to the members of his community, whom we shall call the real readers. So the real author is the personality (or the group) which produces the text. The real reader is the individual or the group for whom the text was originally intended. But the real author and reader are historical figures beyond the reach of the reader who opens the book. They exist outside the text, independently of the text, and can only be reconstructed by historical hypotheses. In the case of biblical literature, the reconstruction of the real authors and readers is the great task carried out by historical criticism; in this documentary quest it tries to imagine from the text who were the circle which produced the Deuteronomistic work, or the author and audience of the Gospels, or the writer and readers of the Apocalypse of John. Now the result of this biographical quest is most often disappointing because of a lack of certainty.

In fact the reconstruction of the author and real readers of any literary work is a fragile and hazardous enterprise. The relationship between an author and his work is dialectical: the author does not put himself entirely into his text. He can give himself a role as narrator which does not correspond to what he really thinks. Narrative fiction authorizes him to develop an imaginary world which does not correspond with his own. In short, to confuse the author and the work is to be as naïve as to take Mickey Mouse as a historical character.

(The notions of story and discourse will be explained later, >2.1.)

Narrator and implied author

It is important to maintain a theoretical distinction between the two notions of narrator and implied author. To put it briefly, the narratologists define the narrator as the voice which guides the reader in the narrative and the implied author as the subject of the narrative strategy. The notion of implied author has been clarified very well by the theoretician Seymour Chatman.

The implied author

This is an aspect of the author which is not a matter for hypothesis or conjecture: the trace that he leaves

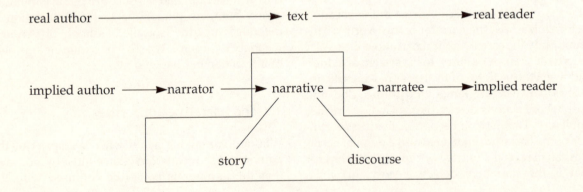

IMPLIED AUTHOR

in the writing of the text. An author is in fact intrinsically present in his work through the choices he makes in writing. If for historical criticism the author is above all a personality whose life needs to be known, narrative criticism works on the notion of author. It distinguishes two approaches.

On the one hand there is the real author, outside the text, the being of flesh and blood whose personality (when it comes to the biblical authors) largely escapes us: the narratologists are not interested in it. On the other hand there is the author who involves himself in his work by his narrative choices: narrative analysis calls him the implied author (a term proposed by W.Booth in *The Rhetoric of Fiction*, in 1961). In fact an author objectifies himself in his work, not by the life that he lives outside it but by the orientation that he gives to his text.

So to seek out the implied author is to discover the narrative strategy that he uses, the choice of style he makes, how he brings in his characters, what system of values the text has. The image of the implied author results from the sum of the choices of writing that are identified in the text. Thus there is an implied author for each literary work; in other words, the image of the author as this is unveiled in this work.

To sum up: narratology redefines the notion of author as a mode of being in the text.

Narrative criticism thus leaves to historical criticism the (risky) task of reconstructing the historical character of the evangelist Matthew. Instead, it sets out to form an image of Matthew as this is suggested through his work, by his well-groomed literary style, his language saturated with Hebrew phrases, his fixation on the question of the Law, the negative role which he attributes to the Pharisees, his positive evaluation of the group of disciples, and so on.

The implied author and the narrator

So far we have given two definitions: the narrator is the voice which guides the reader in the story (> 1.3); the implied author is the subject of the narrative strategy. Seymour Chatman, the first theoretician of narrative criticism, formulates the difference like this: the author is 'implied', i.e. reconstructed by the reader from the story. He is not its narrator, but rather the principle which has invented the narrator, along with the other elements of the narrative: he is the one who has dealt the cards in this particular way, who has wanted such an event to happen to such a character, in these terms or through these images. Given the text, how does the difference function in practice?

It can be that the implied author makes the narrator figure in his text: that is the case at the end of the Fourth Gospel: 'This is the disciple who is bearing witness to these things, and who has written these things; and we know that his testimony is true' (John 21.24). It can be that the implied author creates for himself an untrustworthy narrator from whom he distances himself: this case does not appear in biblical literature, but it does in novels (Agatha Christie's *The Murder of Roger Ackroyd* or Kazuo Ishiguro's *The Remains of the Day*). Umberto Eco has spoken of the narrative trinity which is represented by the author (implied), the narrator and the reader (*Six Walks in the Fictional Woods*, 14).

When this duplication does not take place, we

have to assume that the two terms relate to the same authorial entity, but seen from two different perspectives. He is designated narrator when the implementation of the narrative strategy is evoked. He is designated implied author when the emphasis is on the source of the writing strategy. If we are interested in the author of the First Gospel we will speak of the narrator Matthew to describe the narrative control that he sets in place. We will speak of the implied author Matthew to form a picture of the writer, synthesizing the competences (literary, theological and historical) that he invests in his text. In what follows we shall usually speak of the narrator.

IMPLIED READER

The implied reader

Pragmatic readings are characterized by a transfer of attention from the pole of the author to the pole of the reader; one might expect that narrative criticism would rework the definition of the reader in particular. That has been the case. The orientation of literary criticism on a pragmatics of reading and the advent of the 'era of the reader' have made this notion substantially more complex.

Theoretically, the notion of the implied reader meets up symmetrically with that of the implied author. The same dualism of real/implied is to be found here. The real reader designates either the readership envisaged by the real author when he is writing (the first readers), or every reader faced with the text. The implied reader (Gérard Genette speaks of the virtual reader) is a literary image: every text, envisaging a reader, is inhabited by the image which it has of him. The implied author, in the choices which he makes and which characterizes his narration, acts on the basis of the features that he attributes to this potential reader. For the reader is never just a hypothesis which the writer makes to construct his story, a fictitious entity, an image of the possible reader. This implied reader is the image which has been modelled corresponding to the readership imagined by the author in his work of writing: capacities for knowledge, attitudes, preoccupations, reactions which the author (rightly or wrongly) attributes to his future reader, and which condition the development of his narrative. In the strict sense narratology thus uses the term implied reader to denote a formal position destined to be taken up by the reader.

To know more about the different possible definitions of the implied reader, see Chapter 9 with its box ('The reader in all his states', > 9.1).

The position of narratee is occupied by the receiver of the story, which is symmetrical to the narrator. What has been said of the distinction between narrator and implied author can be repeated here. The narratee can figure explicitly in the text (Mark 13,14: 'Let the reader understand!'); in this case we have an involved narratee. Most often in biblical literature we have an effaced narratee; he is confused with the implied reader, since he is not named, but impliedly present through the knowledge and the values that the narrator presupposes in those to whom the text is addressed.

DEFINITIONS

Real author: the historical character, individual or collective, responsible for the writing of the story; as such he does not touch on the field of narratology.

Real reader: an individual or collective figure representing either the readership for which the real author intends his text (first reader) or everyone engaged in the act of reading. As such this entity does not relate to the field of narratology.

Narrator: the narrative 'voice' from which the narrative comes and the one who relates it.

Narratee: the textual figure of the reader, the narrative authority to whom the narrator addresses his narrative.

Implied author: the image of the author as revealed in the work by its choices of writing and the deployment of a narrative strategy.

Implied reader: the recipient of the narrative constructed by the text and capable of realizing its meanings in the perspective into which the author leads him: this image of the reader corresponds to the readership imagined by the author.

What reader is being spoken of?

Given the blossoming of definitions of the reader in narratology, it is important to control the use of the term. In dealing with biblical narration we shall distinguish three categories of reader.

1. The *first reader-hearer (real)* of the text: this is the contemporary recipient of the real author, for whom he is writing. Historical criticism tries to establish a portrait of the reader from the text, but without being able to check how different this is from the image which the author has of him.

2. *The implied reader:* an abstract reality, the image of the reader addressed by the text. This image can be discovered on the one hand from what the text says (its language, its literary genre, the culture to which it appeals), prescribing a definite reading public; the sense of controversy addressed by the letters of Paul is very different from the taste for a story postulated by a reading of the book of Jonah. The image is then dictated by the instructions for reading, which constitute a kind of co-operative contact between the author and the reader in elaborating the meaning.

3. The *real reader:* you and me faced with the text. This reader is difficult to theorize about, since the parameters which guide his or her reading (cultural, theological or psychological) cannot be foreseen. It must be said that this reader is free in the face of the contract for reading that the text offers. It is also necessary to measure this reader's role in a collective history: his or her individual reading is not only regulated by the reading community to which he or she belongs (Stanley Fish talks of interpretative communities) but is also crossed by previous readings of the text. We do not read the beginning of Genesis independently of the scientific theories of the origin of humankind (whether these are accepted or rejected) or the Sermon on the Mount without any reflection (whether ethical or psychoanalytical) on the law.

1.5 What is a narrative?

It has been said that narrativity is that by which a text or a work can be recognized as narrative (>1.1) But what do we call a 'narrative'? How does a narrative differ from description or discourse? What factors generate what Umberto Eco calls the 'epiphany of narrativity'?

Let's begin with his approach: 'What I mean is that to tell a story you must first of all construct a world, furnished as much as possible, down to the smallest detail' (*Reflections on The Name of the Rose*, 23).This remark is an important one: telling a story is not simply transmitting but constructing a world, the world of the narrative, with its codes and its rules for functioning. But this feature is not enough: a sum of facts does not make a story. Let's continue with T.Todorov: 'Our object is constituted by actions which organize a certain discourse called story' (*Grammaire du Décaméron*, 10). The second feature is that telling a story consists in linking together actions within a causal relationship. That allows us to say that 'she sees a bright blue flower' is a description, while 'she sees a bright blue flower and picks it' is a story; in the second case vision and picking are linked consecutively. But here too the feature is insufficient: the discourse which articulates a relationship of causality in a consecutive way could have been a recipe, or instructions for assembly, just as much as a story.

The third feature is time: Paul Ricoeur's basic intuition in his monumental work *Time and Narrative* is the recognition of the link between causality and temporality as elements of narrativity. 'Everything that is recounted occurs in time, takes time, unfolds temporally, and what unfolds in time can recounted' (*From Text to Action*, 2). If causality distinguishes the narrative from the description, its temporality distinguishes it from the discourse.

In his 'Décrire des actions', J.M.Adam has listed four parameters of the narrative. For it to be a narrative there is a need for:

1. A temporal succession of actions/events;
2. The presence of an agent-hero inspired by an intention which draws the story towards its close;
3. A plot which overhangs the chain of events and integrates them into the unity of a single action;
4. A relationship of causality and consecutiveness which structures the plot by an interplay of causes and effects.

THE BREATH OF THE STORY

'In narrativity, the breathing is derived not from the sentences but from broader units, from the scansion of events' (U.Eco, *Reflections on The Name of the Rose*, 42).

'The common feature of human experience, that which is marked, organized, and clarified by the act of storytelling in all its forms, is its temporal character. Everything that is recounted occurs in time and takes time, unfolds temporally; and what unfolds in time can be recounted. Perhaps indeed, every temporal process is recognized as such only to the extent that it can, in one way or another, be recounted' (P.Ricoeur, *From Text to Action*, 2).

If 'indeed, narrativity is to mark, organize, and clarify temporal experience. . . we must seek in language use a standard of measurement that satisfies this need for delimiting, ordering, and making explicit . . . I shall once again follow Aristotle in his designation of the sort of verbal composition that constitutes a text as narrative. Aristotle designates this verbal composition by use of the term *muthos*, a term that has been translated by "fable" or "plot".'

A story 'must be more than an enumeration of events in serial order; it must organize them into an intelligible whole, of a sort such that we can always ask what is the "thought" of this story. In short, the emplotment is the operation which is that of a configuration out of a simple succession' (P.Ricoeur, *From Text to Action*, 3; *Time and Narrative* I, 65).

For further reading
J. L. Ska, *Our Fathers Have Told Us*, Subsidia Biblica 13, Rome: Pontificio Istituto Biblico 1990, 39–63 (the relationship between narrator and narratee).

This nomenclature makes it possible to establish the indication of narrativity of both a macro-narrative (a historical book, narrative cycle, Gospel) and a micro-narrative (an encounter, miracle, parable etc.). We shall be taking up what is said here about the plot (parameters 3 and 4) in Chapter 4 (> 4.1–2).

Check your knowledge

- What image of the implied reader arises from Judg.1.1–21 in terms of his knowledge, his culture and his experience?
- How does one describe the relationship between narrator and narratee in Rev.1.4–9?

2

Story and discourse

Everyone has experienced it: there are thousands of ways of telling the same story. Modern narratology is built very precisely on this distinction between what is told and the way in which it is told. The aim of this chapter is to set out the reasons, the modes and what is at issue in this distinction. Afterwards it will be necessary to keep it constantly in mind: in this simple demarcation between the 'what' and the 'how' of the narrative is to be found the key to all the procedures, even the most complex, towards this book will lead you.

2.1 A basic distinction

Anyone who tells a story makes a series of important choices, most frequently without being aware of it. How does one begin? Go straight to the point, or set a series of traps to create a dramatic tension? What is to be the setting of the action? Does one establish one of the characters and paint the scene as he sees it? Does one use flashbacks?

> Modern narratology arose out of this distinction between the 'what' of the narrative, what is called the *story*, and the way in which the story is told, which is called its *discourse*.

The narrative takes form in line with the decisions that are taken. Even if the narrator is taking up a well-known plot (for example Little Red Riding Hood), he forms a narrative in his own distinctive style. He will accentuate the cruelty of the

wolf or create auxiliary characters. In the event he will not use his creativity on the 'what' (Little Red Riding Hood) but in the way he tells her story.

Grasping this cardinal distinction between story and discourse is the first step in an introduction to narrative criticism. The story corresponds to the 'events narrated, taken from their setting in the story and reconstructed in their chronological order' (S. Chatman). The story of Little Red Riding Hood can be told in a summary. The discourse is the form given to the narrative by the narrator (= narrativization), which in turn implies a choice of structure, style and disposition. Narratology makes use of differentiated approaches by which it seeks to grasp both of these.

2.2 Story and history must not be confused

A fact of everyday life indicates that the distinction that we have just made between story and discourse is a common one. Several people called to give evidence after a traffic accident will give as many versions of it as there are witnesses. The infinity of possible variants represents so many discourses. Each person in fact expresses his or her particular perspective in the evidence (as a pedestrian, a motorist, a person standing in a particular place).

But we should note that the comparison stops there. For the discrepancy between the witnesses after an accident leads us to postulate an 'authentic' version which can be reconstructed by eliminating

LITTLE RED RIDING HOOD:
ONE STORY, THREE DISCOURSES

the subjective elements which explain the disagreement between the witnesses: this 'reality' would ideally correspond to the police report.

Now the notion of *story* lies on a literary and not a historical level. *Story* has nothing to do with *history*. In other words, the story as it can be reconstructed from the finished project is not to be confused with the 'bare facts', i.e. the events as they really happened. The literary concept of story remains in the story world, without prejudicing its comparison with a historical-type reconstruction.

So the story is the film of events as the narrator has decided to communicate it to the reader (or, if need be, as he imagines it himself). Verification of a historical kind requires documentation external to the narrative, on which narrative criticism cannot pronounce.

2.3 The two elements of the narrative

The *narrative*, in the sense which from now on we shall give to this term, is a material entity: it is the narrative statement that readers have before their eyes or to which hearers listen. Every narrative is made up of two elements: the story and the discourse. Narrative criticism distinguishes these two elements, which cannot be separated in any narrative, in the same way as linguistics differentiates the *signifier* and the *signified*.

A detour (or rather a return) will help us to understand this. Let's return to the linguistic code which we mentioned in connection with Jakobson (>1.1). Ferdinand de Saussure, the father of linguistics, defined the linguistic sign as that which unites not a thing and a name, but a signifier and a signified. The signifier is the phonic or textual expression. The signified is the concept, or, if you like, the semantic content. If we again take the message 'your pear is green', we have said that the context refers to a world of representation (what is a pear, what is the colour green), while the linguistic code allows us to identify the phoneme 'pear'.

We can say the same thing by modifying the terms and adopting the pair signified/signifier. To recognize the word 'pear' (as opposed to 'tear' or 'bear') is to identify the signifier: to understand that it relates to a concept ('pear' as opposed to 'apple' or 'grape') is to identify the signified. When I hear or read 'pear' I relate the signifier 'pear' to the signified 'pear'. The linguistic sign 'pear' thus functions by associating, in a given language, the signifier and signified.

It is the same with narratology, which distinguishes in the narrative between the signified, which is the story that is told, and the signifier, which represents its discourse. The discourse is the result of the work of the narrator, who tells his story from a particular point of view. The whole of the plan adopted by the narrator in the discourse is a choice of narrative rhetoric, i.e. a choice of narrative signifier.

Never one without the other

To separate the signifier from the signified is a useful operation for analysis. But we should remember that a signified never exists without a signifier and vice versa. Moreover the two levels are not watertight. Take, for example, a system of values established by the narrator which distinguishes the 'bad' from the 'good' (see the detective story!); this system is part of narrative rhetoric and leads the narrator to depict some characters as sympathetic and others as antipathetic. But how far can one suppress these connotations while preserving the story? How far can one obliterate the indications of the value-system of the narrator without distorting the story? Our conclusion must be that the separation of story and discourse is necessary for analysis: but the narrative lives on the combination of these two elements.

2.4 The quest for a language

The distinction between the signifier and the signified in a story goes back to Aristotle, who in his

---

DEFINITIONS

Narration: the act or process of producing the narrative.

Narrative: discourse stating facts linked together in a temporal sequence (chronological order) and with a causal link (order of configuration). The narrative is the product of narrative activity.

Story: what the narrative relates, reconstructed in the chronological order which it supposes (the signified).

Discourse: how the story is told (the signifier).

Narrative rhetoric: the totality of the mechanism by which the narrator composes a narrative.

Poetics differentiates *logos* and *muthos* (1449b, 8–9); the Greek philosopher here was distinguishing between direct discourse and the construction of a theatrical plot. But modern narratology has not yet stabilized its vocabulary here: it is still seeking its language.

The Russian formalists (B.Tomachevski) distinguish between *fabula* (story line) and *sjuzet* (plot, discourse). G.Genette (*Figures* III, 1972) suggests the application of the terms *story* (or *diegesis*) and narrative to this duality. S.Chatman (*Story and Discourse*) has formalized the distinction by labelling the 'what' story and the 'how' discourse, which allows him to designate the narrative story-as-discoursed. The Italian A.Marchese (*L'officina del racconto*, 1983) resorts to the opposition between *storia* and *racconto*.

We shall here follow Chatman's suggestion. This terminological distinction avoids the ambivalence often attached to the term narrative: depending on the author, 'narrative' denotes either the production of narrativity by employing a narrative rhetoric (narrative versus diegesis) or the product of this activity (narrative versus drama, treatise, poetry, etc.).

2.5 Discourse and theology

The way a story is told depends on more than one factor: the creativity of the narrator, social conventions, the ideology of the environment, the value system of the social group, and so on. When we come to the biblical narratives, we will note the

---

HOW THEY DEFINE STORY AND NARRATIVE

'I propose to use the term story for the signified or narrative content (even if this context proves in the event to have a weak dramatic intensity or tone), *narrative* in the strict sense for the signifier, statement or narrative text itself, and *narration* for the narrative action of production and, by extension, the whole of the real or fictitious situation in which it takes place' (G. Genette, *Figures* III, 1972, 72).

The story is the *what* (that which is depicted in a narrative); the discourse is the how. . . What is communicated is the story, the element of the narrative attached to the form of the content, and that is communicated by the discourse, the element corresponding to the form of expression… The arrangement is specifically the operation brought about by the discourse. The events of a story are made into a plot by its discourse, the mode or presentation (S.Chatman, *Story and Discourse*, 1978).

For further reading:
G. Genette, *Nouveau discours du récit*, Paris: Editions du Seuil 1983, 10-15 (story and discourse).
M. A. Powell, *What is Narrative Criticism?*, Minneapolis: Fortress Press 1990 (the different elements in the discourse).

important role also played by factors of a social and cultural type and by the theology of the narrator. However, in this last case, rather than individualizing too quickly, we must take account of the group of which the narrator is the spokesman.

Take for example the census ordered by king David. This census is introduced in II Sam.24.1 in these terms: 'The anger of the Lord was kindled against Israel, and he incited David against them, saying, "Go, number Israel and Judah".' Years later, this theology doubtless seemed inadequate to the Chronicler, since he rewrote the passage like this (I Chron.21.1): 'Satan stood up against Israel and incited David to number Israel.'

This comparison of the two stories confirms the theological interest of the distinction between story and discourse. Changing the discourse is not an operation which has to be noted only in literary categories: from the narrator's side, the modification of a narrative structure is built on a theological structure which it is advisable to discover.

When an author wants to take account of a decision which he thinks is disastrous, like the census of Israel by its king, he reinterprets the story told and offers a variant on it. This can be dictated to him by his own theology or by a development of religious sensitivity. Whichever it is, he then enters into communication with the readers to offer them, more or less skilfully, another key for reading than the one that was proposed to them. Bringing out the rhetoric which governs the discourse of the Chronicler, narrative criticism discovers a shift of meaning at the narrative level; it is wise to ask what conviction at the theological level has prompted it.

The narrative strategy

We can already sense that the way in which an episode is related (the discourse) is as important as the events related (the story), if not more so. The role of narrative rhetoric seems so striking to Robert M.Fowler that he can even affirm: 'The success of the story comes about, if it does, not in the story but at the level of discourse' (*Let the Reader Understand*,

258). Applied to the biblical narration, narrative criticism goes back beyond what is said to perceive the modelling used by the author in making the story. If we want to grasp the theology of the narrator, we must essentially question his narrative strategy.

We have seen from the example of the census of Israel how an author can take up a tradition which has been handed down to him, and while keeping an almost identical story can rewrite the text, introducing his own interpretation by an original discourse.

Check your knowledge

- Compare the discourses of the episode 'Jesus enters Jerusalem' in Mark 11.1–10 and John 12.12–19.
- Compare the discourse of the Decalogue according to Ex.19.10-25; 20.8–21 with that according to Deut 5.1–5, 22.

The Synoptic Gospels

A comparison of Mark, Matthew and Luke provides some good examples in which all three keep the story but the discourse changes.

If we compare the three versions of the parable of the wicked husbandmen (Mark 12.1–9; Matt.21.33–41; Luke 20.9–16), while accepting that Matthew and Luke reinterpret the text that they have read in Mark, these later narrators are rewriting a narrative already shaped by Mark. The Matthaean and Lukan versions largely correspond to Mark's narrative in terms of the story; but the work of the later narrators has consisted in partially deconstructing the Markan discourse to insert their own perspective.

To see this compare the three versions of the owner's thought.

Mark 12.6: 'He had still one other, a beloved son; finally he sent him to them, saying, "They will respect my son."'

Matt.21.37: 'Finally he sent his son to them, saying, "They will respect my son."'

Luke 20.13: 'Then the owner of the vineyard said, "What shall I do? I will send my beloved son; it may be that they will respect him."'

The variants, even the tiny ones (the 'still one other' of Mark, the 'finally' of Matthew, and the 'perhaps' of Luke) conceal subtle nuances of meaning… The same story goes the rounds, from Mark to Matthew and Luke, but the discourse of the text-source has been partially destroyed and remodelled by the second narratives.

An application: Jesus walks on the water (Mark 6.45–53; Matt.14.22–34; John 6.16–21)

The three variants of this episode in Mark, Matthew and John allow us to see more precisely how the distinction between story and discourse operates.

Narrative criticism is interested in grasping how without the story being notably retouched, three evangelists each come to compose a specific narrative, simply by the differentiated play of their narrative strategy. We also see that their narrative strategy is at the service of a theology: in Mark it points to the progressive isolation of Jesus, in Matthew to the paradigmatic relationship between master and disciples, while John is concerned to present the enigma of the one sent by God.

The story (according to Mark). If, beginning from Mark's narrative, we go back to the story, we get an episode in four scenes.

First scene. Jesus asks his disciples to get back on board ship and go before him to the other side.

Mark 6.45 Immediately Jesus made his disciples get into the boat and go before him to the other side, to Bethsaida, while he dismissed the crowd. 46 And after he had taken leave of them, he went into the hills to pray. 47 And when evening came, the boat was out on the sea, and he was alone on the land. 48 And he saw that they were distressed in rowing, for the wind was against them. And about the fourth watch of the night he came to them, walking on the sea. He meant to pass by them, 49 but when they saw him walking on the sea they though it was a ghost, and cried out; 50 for they all saw him, and were terrified. But immediately he spoke to them and said, 'Take heart, it is I; have no fear.' 51 And he got into the boat with them and the wind ceased. And they were utterly astounded, 52 for they did not understand about the loaves, but their hearts were hardened.	**Matthew** 14.22 Then he made the disciples get into the boat and go before him to the other side, while he dismissed the crowds. 23 And after he had dismissed the crowds, he went up into the hills by himself to pray. When evening came, he was there alone; 24 but the boat by this time was many furlongs distant from the land, beaten by the waves; for the wind was against them. 25 And in the fourth watch of the night he came to them, walking on the sea. They were terrified, saying, 'It is a ghost!' And they cried out for fear. 27 But immediately he spoke to them, saying, 'Take heart, it is I; have no fear.' 28 And Peter answered him, 'Lord, if it is you, bid me come to you on the water.' 29 He said, 'Come.' So Peter got out of the boat and walked on the water and came to Jesus; 30 but when he saw the wind, he was afraid, and beginning to sink he cried out, 'Lord, save me.' 31 Jesus immediately reached out his hand and caught him, saying to him, 'O man of little faith, why did you doubt?' 32 And when they got into the boat, the wind ceased. 33 And those in the boat worshipped him, saying, 'Truly you are the Son of God.'	**John** 6.16 When evening came, his disciples went down to the sea, 17 got into a boat, and started across the sea to Capernaum. It was now dark, and Jesus had not yet come to them. 18 The sea rose because a strong wind was blowing. 19 When they had rowed for about three of four miles, they saw Jesus walking on the sea and drawing near to the boat. They were frightened, 20 but he said to them, 'It is I, do not be afraid.' 21 Then they were glad to take him into the boat, and immediately the boat was at the land to which they were going.

He himself dismisses the crowd and goes alone into the hills.

Second scene. Night has fallen and the disciples are struggling laboriously against a headwind.

Third scene. Jesus comes to them walking on the sea. When they see him they begin to cry out.

Fourth scene. Jesus reassures them, telling them: 'Have faith, it is I, do not be afraid.' Then he gets into the boat with them and the wind falls. The disciples are overwhelmed by this.

The discourse in Mark. To detect the discourse used by Mark is to see how he unfolds the event and what procedures he uses to guide the reader in this narrative communication.

A painter could emphasize the withdrawal of Jesus, alone on the mountains while the disciples in the distance are struggling with their oars. In the cinema, a director would bring out the miraculous, dwelling on the progressive appearance of Jesus, under the eyes of the disciples grappling with the storm. Mark takes another approach. He chooses to associate the course of the reader with that of Jesus, in order to detach the reader from the disciples. At the beginning of the narrative we learn that Jesus asks his disciples to get back into the boat. Then the reader follows Jesus so to speak step by step: dismissing the crowd, going alone into the mountain (we even have access to his intention, 'to pray'), watching the disciples' struggle with the elements that have been unleashed, going to meet them (we again have access to his intention: 'he wanted to overtake them').

The break which comes about at v.49 then occurs with full force: the fact of being so closely linked with what Jesus has been doing leads the readers to distance themselves from the disciples: in their eyes it is clear that Jesus in person, and not a phantom, is appearing to them. Even after Jesus has revealed his identity ('Take heart, it is I, have no fear') the disciples are still overcome. This state could surprise the reader, since Jesus has rejoined them in the ship and the wind has fallen. Mark has to explain it, and he gives two reasons: 'for they did not understand about the loaves, but their hearts were hardened' (v.52). The theme of a failure to understand and a hardening (a reminder of the exodus from Egypt) indicates that a gulf has been created between Jesus and his disciples which will continue to widen in subsequent chapters. Mark here lets a major preoccupation of his story come through: how is Jesus known?

The discourse in Matthew. The story told by Matthew is very close to that of Mark, except for the addition of a scene in which Peter suggests to Jesus that he should meet him on the water (vv.28–31).

In the discourse we can see that the disciples have a very different role from that in Mark. They are terrified (v.26), but neither obtuse nor hardened. The inserted scene presents, in the person of Peter, a sympathetic figure of a disciple, overcoming the general terror but trapped by fear (v.30). The reader will easily recognize in this character in whom trust and fear are mixed the believer of 'little faith' to whom Jesus stretches out his hand to save his life. The relationship between the reader and the figure of the disciples is created round an identification rather than a distancing. And we can understand why the story ends in terms which are different from, if not opposed to, those of the Second Gospel: the disciples hail Jesus as Son of God (v.33). The climate is at the opposite extreme since half-way through (v.28) the reader has been led to leave Jesus' course to follow that of Peter.

The discourse in John. The author of the Fourth Gospel has on the one hand chosen the course of stripping the narrative in an extreme way: the narrative accelerates to its enigmatic denouement (v.21). He has equally firmly associated the reader with the group of disciples labouring in the boat: they are the ones who have decided to make the crossing (v.16), who are rowing in the darkness and facing the storm, who see Jesus and take fright. After Jesus has reassured them, they are again the ones who *wanted to take him into the boat* (v.21). The reader, so to speak taken into the boat with them, is completely associated with their terror.

MAX WAS SHORT BECAUSE
AN ANVIL HAD FALLEN
ON HIS HEAD

HEY, MAX, WHAT
HAPPENED TO YOU?

AN ANVIL FELL
ON MY HEAD

EXTRADIEGETIC AUTHORITY

The denouement is all the more surprising. John does not say that Jesus gets into the boat and that the wind drops. When the disciples plan to take him on board, the boat reaches land! John's story does not culminate in either a remark about hardening or the acclamation of the disciples; on the contrary, the narrator shows Jesus getting out of the grips of his disciples. In complete contrast to the Markan account, Jesus' course in John remains a total enigma here.

2.6 The different positions of the narrator

Where does the 'voice' which relates the narrative come from?

A narrator can begin with the words, 'A man had two sons...' The 'voice' is drowned by the story, and can be perceived only by the orchestration of the narrative plan. But the narrator can also begin by saying, 'I am going to tell you the story of the man who had two sons...' The 'voice' then emerges in the story which it is telling, making a space for itself by the narrator's 'I'.

The term *narrative authority* is used to describe the status that the narrator gives himself in the relationship with the text: this status can vary in accordance

INTRADIEGETIC AUTHORITY

with a taxonomy which runs from complete effacement (descriptive narrative) to total presence (autobiographical narrative). The criterion used to describe narrative authority is the relationship between the narrator and the story, which can also be called *diegesis* (G.Genette's term). Diegesis (or the story told) is the spatio-temporal universe unfolded in the story. But this relationship can be envisaged under two different perspectives.

In the face of the story told

Let's establish a first distinction. The narrator can put himself outside or inside the story told. If he is outside, the term used is *extradiegetic* authority: that is the case with Mark, author of the Second Gospel, who never puts himself into his narrative. Or the narrator is inside, and then the term used is *intradiegetic* authority. That is the case with Jesus telling a parable: but he figures as the narrator narrated, i.e. the secondary narrator (whose words are reported by an extradiegetic narrator, a primary narrator, who is the evangelist).

Intrusive narrator

Let's establish a second distinction. The narrator can decide not to disguise his presence at the narra-

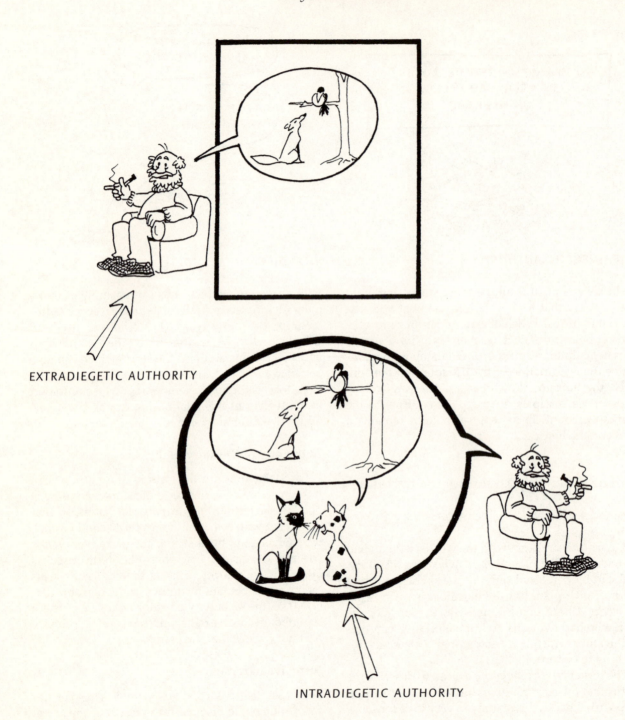

EXTRADIEGETIC AUTHORITY

INTRADIEGETIC AUTHORITY

tive level: then his intrusion can take two forms. In the first case it relates to events in which he does not intervene and does not figure (for example, the narrator Luke intrudes into his narrative in Luke 1.1–4 but does not figure in the Gospel between Luke 1 and Luke 24): this is called *heterodiegetic*. But the narrator can make himself present in the story which he tells, thus making himself *homodiegetic*: that is the case with the narrator Luke, author of the Acts of the Apostles, in the four 'we' sequences in Acts (16.10-17; 20.5–15; 21.1–18; 27.1–28.16).

This brings us to a combination of four elements. But we must not fail to note that while the two distinctions can be combined, they lie on different levels. The first opposition expresses itself on a question of level: if one looks at the *story told*, the narrator is inside or outside. For example, in Matt.13 (the parables chapter) the evangelist is not part of the story, so he is extradiegetic, while Jesus is an intradiegetic (second) narrator. The other opposition relates to the relationship between the narrator and *the story which he tells*: he is absent from or present in his narrative discourse. For example, Mark and Matthew are heterodiegetic narrators, unlike the author of the Acts of the Apostles and the author of the Apocalypse.

Crossed characteristics

To be even more subtle, it must be added that the situation can get yet more complicated. A narrator can be both present in the story (intradiegetic) while telling a story from which he is absent (heterodiegetic).

In Isaiah 38 the author of the narrative (who is none other than the prophet himself) mentions the sickness of King Hezekiah and his own approach to the king: here we have a narrator who is both extradiegetic and homodiegetic at the same time, even if he is speaking of himself in the third person. This is a status diametrically opposed to that in Gen.41.14–36, where Joseph, a character in the narrative, gives Pharaoh his interpretation of the dream – which does not imply (or does not yet imply) himself. Here Joseph is an intradiegetic and a heterodiegetic authority.

A last point: do not confuse the 'voice' which relates the narrative (the answer to the question *who is relating the narrative*?) with the point of view adopted by the narrator (question: *who perceives the event in the narrative*?). In John 6.16–21, the 'voice' is that of the author of the Fourth Gospel; on the other hand the narrator has chosen to tell the event of the crossing of the lake by adopting the perspective of

---

Check your knowledge

- What is the status of the narrator Nathan in II Sam.12.1–15?
- What is the status of the narrator Peter in Acts 10.34–43?
- What is the status of the narrator John in Revelation 1.9–20?

DEFINITIONS

Diegesis (another term for 'story'): the spatial-and-temporal universe unfolded by the narrative.

On the level of activity of the narrator

Extradiegetic: external to the story (primary narrator).

Intradiegetic: internal to the story (secondary narrator).

On the relationship between the narrator and the story told

Homodiegetic: said of a narrator present in the story that he relates.

Heterodiegetic: said of a narrator absent from the story that he relates.

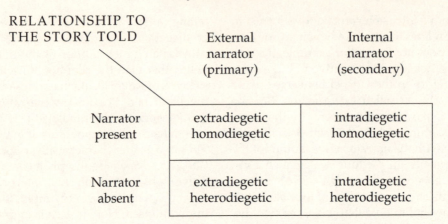

RELATIONSHIP TO
THE STORY TOLD

	External narrator (primary)	Internal narrator (secondary)
Narrator present	extradiegetic homodiegetic	intradiegetic homodiegetic
Narrator absent	extradiegetic heterodiegetic	intradiegetic heterodiegetic

the disciples in the boat. Here we remain at the level of 'the voice', i.e. of the narrator. The question of perspective will be touched on later (> 5.8).

For further reading
G. Genette, *Nouveau discours du récit*, Paris: Editions du Seuil 1983, 77–89 (intradiegetic/extradiegetic).
D. Marguerat, *Le Dieu des premiers chrétiens*, Geneva: Labor et Fides [3]1997 (theology as narrative).

Albrecht Dürer (1471–1528), *The throne and the elders*.

3

The closure of the narrative

Where does a narrative begin and where does it end? The simple decision by which a reader begins to read at a particular point and ends at a particular point is a choice of considerable importance. What criteria do readers rely on to cut out in the flesh of the text a narrative segment that they will call 'narrative'? Doesn't cutting the thread of the narration to extract a piece in any case do violence to the text?

The structuralists were the first to want to bring this operation under control. For to delimit the text to be read, *to establish its closure*, gives the story a beginning and an end: and this decision already involves the meaning of the narrative. The proof of this is that to strip a narrative of its final twist or to ignore what makes it get off the ground is completely to distort it. To cut too early or too late is to disfigure the narrative.

To decide the closure of the text is a first interpretative act which, by marking out a unit that makes sense, opens the reading and programmes its regulation.

3.1 Jesus and Nicodemus

Let's pause on chapter 3 of the Gospel of John. The reading of the encounter between Jesus and Nicodemus can begin at verse 1, as usual, and there are good reasons for this:

(a) we are at the beginning of a chapter;

(b) Nicodemus appears for the first time in the story in 3.1; and

(c) this verse presents Nicodemus with a formula-tion which suggests the beginning of a narrative: 'Now there was a man of the Pharisees, named Nicodemus, a ruler of the Jews.'

But to what does this little particle 'now' relate? Going back in the text, we see that the end of chapter 2 speaks of the many 'who believed in his *name because of the signs which he did*. But Jesus did not trust himself to them since he knew all men' (2.23b-24). How does Nicodemus approach Jesus? Precisely by saying to him: 'Rabbi, we know that you are a master who comes from God, for no one *can do the signs that you do* unless God is with him' (3.2b).

So Nicodemus comes to Jesus because of the signs which he is performing, and sign is the Johannine term for miracle; but just beforehand the narrator has indicated that Jesus mistrusts those who believe in him *because of the signs*. Here the reader is warned: Nicodemus is advancing into a minefield! How is the conversation to develop on the basis of this critical information? How will Nicodemus go on? Where will the approach that the previous verses suggest end up?

So from the start the readers are informed of what is at issue in this encounter. . . at least if they have established the closure earlier in the narrative in John 2.23 rather than in 3.1! But what signal has warned them to go back earlier than 3.1? What narrative indicator has made them understand that the motive of the dialogue between Jesus and this prominent Pharisee was to be sought earlier? Attention to the procedures of making a closure prove necessary if we want to objectify the decision

---

DEFINITIONS

Closure: the totality of narrative indicators which fix a beginning and an end to the narrative, thus delimiting a space where meaning is produced.

Making a closure: the operation by which the narrator marks the two extremes of the text to establish its frontiers.

---

to make a cut by which the reading chooses a territory.

3.2 In search of criteria

Making a closure in the text can easily be found from formal marks (make-up, white spaces in the typography, etc.). Modern novels give the reader signs by cutting their text into chapters; these massive breaks function to warn of the end of an episode and the beginning of a new one. Now in the biblical text the structuring in chapters is not a trustworthy indication.

Neither chapters nor verses

It is necessary to know that the division of the text into chapters does not go back to the biblical authors, nor does the division into verses. When copied on scrolls and codices by the copyists, for more than a thousand years the text was presented in continuous form. For the Hebrew Bible, the first traces of a division into verses go back to the scribes of the Talmudic period (fifth century), but it was not until 1553 that their numbering was adopted. For the New Testament, the numbering of the chapters goes back to the efforts of the Englishman Stephen Langton (1203). The distribution into verses appears for the first time in the edition of the Greek text by the Geneva publisher Robert Estienne in 1551, and from then on was authoritative. But the criteria used for this numbering of the text are practical: they reflect the reading of the theologians and the Greek scholars, and take no account of narrativ-

ity. The biblical author did not have chapters or verses to mark the internal frontiers of the story: only means of a narrative kind allowed him to suggest the desirable closures to the readers.

A chain of episodes

It is true that reading habits lead us quite spontaneously to isolate a piece of text. The publishers of our Bibles help us by cutting the text into little narrative blocks, headed by a title. This procedure corresponds to a state of affairs: without exception, the narrative material in the Bible does not present long narratives displaying the kind of continuity that we find in a novel by Dickens. The biblical narrative is made up more of a succession of episodes, sometimes short and sometimes long, the consecutive reading of which does not suppress the impression of a chopped up narrative.

If we look at the first chapter of the Gospel of Mark, we shall see that in its 45 verses it lines up no fewer than ten little episodes. The *Good News Bible* has given this chapter ten titles: *John the Baptist* (vv.1–8), *the baptism of Jesus* (vv.9–11), *the temptation of Jesus in the wilderness* (vv.12–13), *Jesus preaches the gospel in Galilee* (vv.14–15), *the calling of four fishermen* (vv.16–20), *Jesus manifests his authority in the synagogue in Capernaum* (vv.21–28), *healing of Peter's mother-in-law* (vv.29–31), *healings on the sabbath* (vv.32–24), *Jesus leaves Capernaum* (vv.35–39), *cleansing of a leper* (vv.40–45).

Source criticism (which seeks to identify the traditions collected by an author) explains the reasons for this chopping up; it tells us that this chain of episodes brings together a number of elements which were initially autonomous, that the evangelist has fused them together to compose his long narrative. Among these old elements reused by the author we can identify a summary of preaching, an exorcism, a healing story, a biographical narrative, and so on. But if this genealogical analysis indicates what Mark has composed this chapter from, it does not yet tell us how the evangelist has organized his narrative, making use of these elements. To identify the pre-existing material does not tell us anything about the structure that the narrator has given to his text.

So the fragmentation into paragraphs suggested by the publishers of our Bibles is too orientated on criteria of a literary or genealogical order for us to be able to retain them from a narrative point of view.

The conclusion must be that neither the markers (chapters, verses, titles) provided by our Bibles nor a genealogical inquiry can provide certain indications for structuring the text. If we want to go forward in a less random way we must look for narrative indicators of the making of a closure.

3.3 The indicators of closure

The closure of a text is an important factor in the production of meaning, since it selects some relationships for the reader and excludes others. In connection with the episode of Nicodemus we have seen the effect of the proximity of John 2.23–24 and 3.2 (> 3.1).

The narrator has four parameters for marking out a particular narrative episode (we shall call it a *micro-narrative*) in a literary work (which we shall call a *macro-narrative*): the time, the place, the constellation of characters and the theme.

The criterion of time lists the changes of chronology (the next day, several years later, six days before Passover, etc.)

The criterion of place indicates modifications in space (set out, go abroad, leave the house, enter a synagogue).

The criterion of characters lists the changes in the constellation of the actors in the narrative: the appearance or disappearance of a character or a group of characters.

The fourth criterion is additional: a theme can function as the unifying principle of a narrative and maintain its unity through the changes of place or time. It is this last criterion which led us to adopt the first closure before the conversation with Nicodemus in John 2.23 rather than in 3.1 (the unifying theme is 'see the signs and believe', 2.23 and 3.2).

Caution will lead us to add together two or three criteria rather than to pronounce the closure of a micro-narrative on the basis of a single criterion. The difficulty in finding a second criterion to fix a closure reveals that the micro-narrative is part of a narrative sequence (several micro-narratives added together) and that this sequence has indications of continuity hierarchically superior to the indications of closure in the episode. We shall be returning to this later (> 3.4).

Clean closures...

The narrative of the binding of Isaac (Gen.22.1–19) can easily be demarcated. The indicators of closure are clean: an indication of time ('now after these events'); God's order to go to another place (the country of Moriah); a selection of characters (Abraham takes two of his young men and his son). The theme is specific, even completely original: Abraham, on the Lord's orders, is ready to sacrifice Isaac, the son of the promise. At the end of the narrative (v.19) Abraham establishes himself at Beersheba. The micro-narrative which follows (22.20–24) begins with a new indication of time identical to v. 1 ('now after these events') and tells of births in the form of a genealogy which extends the group of characters. Other examples of clean closures are the three young men in the furnace (Dan.3: place, time, characters, theme), or Jacob's struggle with the angel (Gen.32.23–33: place, nomination of characters, theme).

. . . and threads

Even in the case of clean closures, however, it is necessary always to be attentive to the threads which link the episodes together in the narrative chain.

Thus in the case of the narrative of the miraculous catch of fish told in Luke 5.1–11, it is not difficult to find the making of the closure with the help of a new place (the story leaves the desert for Lake Gennesaret and its shore), time (it is 'the day when the people pressed upon him to hear the word of God'), and a new constellation of characters (the crowd by the lakeside and the crew of Simon's boat have replaced 'the crowds' pursuing Jesus in the wilderness in 4.42). The theme is specific: a failed fishing trip miraculously overcome by obedience to the word of Jesus.

Now a thematic thread links this episode (micronarrative) to the story which includes it (macronarrative): the motif of the word. The process is certainly discrete. But if we read attentively, this motif runs through the chain of the narrative linking 4.42–44 (Jesus wants to preach the good news elsewhere) to 5.15 (the crowds gather to hear him), passing through the heart of this episode (Simon acts 'on the word' of Jesus: 5.5). Bringing together these successive episodes, the theme of the word preached and its effectiveness overhangs the fragmentation of the scenes and suggests a discreet scarlet thread to the reader.

Attention paid to the narrative threads picks up the traditional emphasis on the literary 'context', but it takes the analysis further and puts it on a pragmatic level (an investigation of the effects on the reader). It is not just a matter of listing what frames the story on either side. It is important to find indications of continuity (and to hold on to them), relating to a narrative scenario of which the narrative constitutes a particular stage. In fact, in the course of reading, readers never come completely fresh to a particular story: they are full of all that the narrator has made them hear and understand previously. Discovering narrative threads shows which situation, which elements are going to

be pursued by the story, and which abandoned (perhaps provisionally) by the narrator.

New twists in the story and the narrator's trick

As we have said, reading habits play their part. For example, they lead us to stop a narrative where we think it appropriate, particularly where it 'ends well'. Now the narrator may be more subtle than ending on a happy ending, and give his story a new twist beyond the expected ending.

Such a trick is to be supposed in the construction of the story of Naaman and Elisha (II Kings 5). The narrative begins at the court of the king of Aram with the leprosy of general Naaman (5.1). It lists the vicissitudes through which this valiant warrior will be led until he takes the promise of Elisha seriously, humbles himself, and plunges into the Jordan to be purified. But where do we put the closure at the end of the story?

A first hypothesis is that it should be put at v.19a, when on being asked whether Naaman can take a bit of the soil of Israel back to Aram, Elisha replies by blessing Naaman with the wish for *shalom*: 'Go in peace.' The general, healed, can return home. Now the narrative continues by introducing a new character in v.20, Gehazi, Elisha's servant. Is this a new episode or a continuation? The action is going to revolve round this new protagonist, with his attempt to gain favours from Naaman and the terrible punishment which follows: Naaman's leprosy falls on Gehazi and his descendants (v.27).

If the reading stops at 19a, the narrative tells the story of Naaman and ends with the return of the man healed; 19b-27 is just a tragic appendix. If we find a closure in verses 1 and 27, the narrative unfolds a different story: the course of the leprosy, which withdraws from the one who recognizes the God of Israel, though he is a stranger, and returns to one who observes God's rights, though he is a son of the covenant. The narrator has controlled his surprise well, surreptitiously introducing a secondary character to add a final barb to the narrative. But this extension of the network of characters by the insertion of Gehazi does not endanger the continuity of the story; this is safeguarded by the criteria of place (return to Aram), time (v.19b) and theme (the recognition of the author of the healing).

Check your knowledge

- Does the narrative of Saul's conversion in Acts 9 end in 9.19a, 9.25 or 9.30? What criteria can be used for making the closure?
- Suggest a closure for the famous story of Cain and Abel (Gen.4).

3.4 The scenes

A narrative episode is most often made up of successive scenes like a film. Structuring a micro-narrative amounts to identifying the scenes of which it is composed. The transition from one scene to another comes about through a change of character or a change of place or a change of time or a change of perspective (we can imagine the movement of a camera, changing location or perspective, zooming in or pulling out). However, here again one indicator is rarely enough; it is desirable to be sure that at least two criteria converge.

So in structuring a micro-narrative it is necessary to pay less attention to the words exchanged than to the way in which the event is controlled: the framework, the image composed by the narrator. The scene changes when the narrator makes the readers see something else, when he offers them another overall view or another segment of it.

Presenting a spectacle

It is no exaggeration to say that chapter 4 of the Revelation of St John shows readers a spectacle. The narrator makes them share in the vision of the seer of the Apocalypse: a grandiose panorama of the throne of God and the heavenly liturgy.

Looking at the composition of the narrative closely, one admires the precision of the narrative control. The micro-narrative unfolds a series of little scenes as if, put before a gigantic spectacle, the camera was panning round, stopping successively at a number of places to show the readers their meaning.

The description moves away from the throne on a centrifugal trajectory, bringing in the four living creatures and relating their singing to the adoration of the elders. So the narrator has arranged a guided tour of the heavenly world, choosing his itinerary, and in passing showing what he wanted to show. There is no doubt that the order of the scenes and their composition corresponds to a very precise theological plan: the vision of the one 'sitting on the throne', which appeals to mineral images, presents a transcendent God, the source of life but beyond the vicissitudes of human history; on the rebound, the liturgy passes from the throne to the elders, then to the angels, and goes on to encompass the whole world (5.13).

DEFINITIONS

Macro-narrative: the maximal narrative unit conceived of as a whole by the narrator. Example: a Gospel or a historical book (Joshua).

Micro-narrative: the minimal narrative unit presenting a narrative episode the unity of which can be identified by the indicators of closure.

Narrative sequence: a series of micro-narratives linked by a unifying theme or a common character.

Scene: sub-unit of a micro-narrative.

APOCALYPSE 4.1–11

Scene 1 (v.1): the seer is taken up into heaven.
Scene 2 (vv.2–3): the divine throne, the centre of the spectacle.
Scene 3 (vv.4–6a): around the throne the twenty-four elders, the seven spirits and the sea.
Scene 4 (vv.6b-8): the four living creatures and their song.
Scene 5 (vv.9–11): the adoration of the twenty-four elders triggered off by the praise of the four living creatures.

Having probed the sub-unit of the micro-narrative, the scene, let us turn to the entity that is hierarchically superior: the sequence.

3.5 The narrative sequence

Sequence is the term applied to a narrative unit composed of several micro-narratives, linked by a common theme or by the presence of the same principal character. The identification of a sequence can be an important contribution to reading, since it makes one grasp how the narrator constructs his character or his theme, and then, the contribution of each micro-narrative in this architecture.

The heroes

The Hebrew Bible is well known for its sequences constructed round a hero: Abraham, Deborah, Gideon, Samson, Elijah, Elisha. In reading sequences involving characters we should note carefully how the narrator progressively constructs this character. How is he presented? How does he develop?

AS AT THE CINEMA – THE CRUCIFIXION OF JESUS

The narrator can construct his micro-narrative in the same way as a film director, alternating close-ups, middle-distance shots and wide shots; these last correspond to the panoramic view. That is how the evangelist Mark makes us present at the drama of the Passover: the episode of the crucifixion (15.21–41) consists of a scrupulous alignment of successive shots. This is how he presents them in the text.

Wide shot
Middle-distance shot
Close-up
15.21 *And they compelled a passer-by, Simon of Cyrene, who was coming in from the country, the father of Alexander and Rufus, to carry his cross.* 22 And they brought him to the place called Golgotha (which means the place of a skull). 23 *And they offered him wine mingled with myrrh; but he did not take it.* 24 And they crucified him, and divided his garments among them, casting lots for them, to decide what each should take.

25 And it was the third hour, when they crucified him. 26 And the inscription of the charge against him read, 'The King of the Jews.' 27 And with him they crucified two robbers, one on his right and one on his left. 29 And those who passed by derided him, wagging their heads, and saying, 'Aha! You who would destroy the temple and build it in three days, 30 save yourself, and come down from the cross!'

31 So also the chief priests mocked him to one another with the scribes, saying, 'He saved others; he cannot save himself. 32 Let the Christ, the King of Israel, come down now from the cross, that we may see and believe.' Those who were crucified with him also reviled him.

33 And when the sixth hour had come, there was darkness over the whole land until the ninth hour. **34 And at the ninth hour Jesus cried with a loud voice, 'Eloi, Eloi, lama sabachthani?', which means, 'My God, my God, why have you forsaken me?'** 35 And some of the bystanders hearing it said, 'Behold, he is calling Elijah.' 36 And one ran and, filling a sponge full of vinegar, put it on a reed and gave it to him to drink, saying, 'Wait, let us see whether Elijah will come to take him down.' 37 And Jesus uttered a loud cry, and breathed his last. 38 And the curtain of the temple was torn in two, from top to bottom.

39 *And when the centurion, who stood facing him, saw that he thus breathed his last, he said, 'Truly this man was Son of God!'* 40 There were also women looking on from afar, among whom were Mary Magdalene, and Mary the mother of James the younger and of Joses, and Salome, 41 who, when he was in Galilee, followed him, and ministered to him; and also many other women who came up with him to Jerusalem.

CLOSE-UP   MIDDLE-DISTANCE SHOT   WIDE SHOT

What transformations does he undergo? What is his programme?

The Deborah cycle is a closed sequence in the book of Judges (4.1–5.31). From her appearance in the narrative, Deborah is presented as a prophetess judging in Israel (4.4), while the people is oppressed by Jabin king of Canaan. She is the one who takes the initiative in summoning Barak and decides to attack the oppressor; when Barak asks for her support, she is the one who prophesies that God will give the victory through a woman, Jael (4.9; cf. vv.17–22), and again she is the one who gives the order to attack. When the song of victory rings out (Judg.5), the reader is not surprised to learn the title which is given to her, 'mother in Israel' (5.7).

The biblical authors readily resort to a change of title or name to indicate the new status acquired by the hero of the sequence. Jacob becomes Israel (Gen.32.29), Cephas becomes Peter (Matt.16.18) and Saul becomes Paul (Acts 13.9).

Thematic sequences

It is not as easy to isolate a thematic sequence as it is to isolate a sequence of characters, since the theme is a more fluid narrative entity. The difficulty is not very great for the major sequences: the cycle of plagues in Egypt (Ex.7.8–11.10) precedes that of the exodus (Ex.12.1–15.20); the episodes of I Samuel 4.2–7.1 cluster around the ark of the covenant; and Judges 1–12 clusters round the entry into Canaan.

The shortest sequences are held together by the least obvious links. To discover them it is necessary in the first place to pay attention to the closures in the same way as one marks out a micro-narrative: what are the signs of the opening and the closing of the sequence? If the recurrence of the theme is noted, watch how it goes: how does it develop from one end of the sequence to the other? Finally, discover how the various episodes are linked within the sequence: what kind of sequential linking is this? Episodes can be linked in various ways: the link can be linear, i.e. the sequence is presented as a chain of micro-stories; it can also be more sophisticated and be made up of inclusions, forming a 'sandwich'.

Let's look at the evangelist Mark, the champion of sequential construction. Three examples teach us how a thematic sequence is composed, how it constructs its programme, and what in narratology is called a 'sandwich'.

Mark's way

The fragmentation of the narrative of the Second Gospel into a myriad of micro-narratives is only apparent. In reality the narrator has been engaged in weaving subtle narrative connections which link these fragments together in such a way that the plot never stops rebounding from one to the other.

In the middle of his narrative, between 8.27 and 10.52, Mark has constructed the 'sequence of the way'. It takes its name from the many reminders with which the text is strewn that Jesus and the disciples are 'on the way' (8.27; 9.33,34; 10.17, 32, 34, 46, 52). The sequence thus presents a geographical shift, and this shift is no trivial one, since it takes the group from Galilee (8.27) to Jerusalem (11.1), where the story of the passion is to begin.

The indications of closure are as imposing as the pillars of a gateway. They comprise two narratives about the healing of a blind man. The first precedes the sequence (8.22–26); it is strange because the healing takes place in two stages, and Jesus has to repeat himself, as if the blindness was particularly difficult to conquer. The second concludes the sequence (10.46–52): Bartimaeus is healed because he insists and overcomes the resistance of the crowd around Jesus: 'Immediately he regained his sight and followed Jesus on the way' (10.52). From one side of the sequence to the other, we have moved from a laborious healing to an immediate rehabilitation. By what effect?

The symbolic dimension of the way leaps out: it is the place where the Master is followed and his word is heard. Furthermore, with the exception of the debate on marriage (10.1–12), the opponents of Jesus are absent: only Jesus, the disciples and the crowd give life to the sequence. On the way, Jesus is listened to.

The sequence is emphasized by three announcements of the suffering and resurrection of Christ: 8.31; 9.31; 10.32–34. But after each announcement there is a misunderstanding; in other words, the announcement of the suffering is followed by an intervention showing that the disciple have not understand what the passion is about. Peter scolds Jesus, who warns him of his imminent death (8.32f.); the disciples compete over the question of power (9.33–37); James and John ask to share the honours of the kingdom with Jesus (10.35–45). Mark clearly constructs the sequence with the aim of contrasting attitudes.

Seen close-up, this play of oppositions and paradoxes dominates the whole passage. The reader passes straight from the mystic heights of the transfiguration to the distress awaiting Jesus and his disciples at the foot of the mountain (9.2–29). The rivalry over who is the greatest leads Jesus to speak of the little ones (9.33–50). Immediately after introducing children (10.13–16), the story brings in a rich man (10.17). The request to sit with Jesus in his glory (10.37) immediately precedes the story of Bartimaeus, who imploringly insists, 'Son of David, have mercy on me' (10.47f.). High and low, riches and poverty, strength and weakness, ambition and humility: the sequence of the way is constructed on these oppositions. Only readers who accept these paradoxes will succeed, like Bartimaeus, in seeing and following: 'If anyone would follow me, let him deny himself and take up his cross and follow me' (8.34).

A story about loaves

As we can see with the two healings of a blind man which mark the edges of the sequence of the way, the repetition of a narrative episode can be a good indication of a sequence. Readers will find this procedure again in Mark's sequence of the loaves (Mark 6.30–8.21). It owes its name to the presence of two stories about the multiplication of loaves (6.30–44 and 8.1–10) and the resurgence of the motive of bread in 6.52; 7.27f. and 8.14–20. Readers classically have difficulties with this repetition: why two stories the formulation of which is so similar? How are we to understand this repetition?

Source criticism answers the question by trying to identify two different narrative traditions collected by the evangelist. Narrative criticism shifts the question from *why* to *how*. How does the author organize the narrative move from one story to the other?

It is fruitful to note the geographical indications. Where are each of these two miracles of plenty performed? In chapter 6, in a desert place to which Jesus withdraws with his disciples on the shores of Lake Gennesaret (6.32–34). In chapter 8 the story is set elsewhere: in the territory of the Decapolis (7.31), the majority of the population of which is non-Jewish. From Mark 6 to Mark 8 we pass from Israel to Gentile territory. If the first multiplication of the loaves is destined for Jewish crowds and the second for non-Jewish crowds, how does the transfer take place? Jesus' encounter with the Syro-Phoenician woman, put mid-way between the two episodes (7.24–30), provides the key. For this woman, who is not a Jew, protests at Jesus' refusal to give the 'children's bread' to the dogs; she exclaims, 'True Lord, but the dogs under the table eat the children's crumbs' (7.28). Jesus' acceptance of the woman's argument (7.29) prepares the reader to hear the story of the miracle of plenty once again, knowing that the woman's faith has ensured that the children's bread is shared with those excluded from the table.

Check your knowledge

- Divide into scenes the narrative of the appearance to Abraham by the oaks of Mamre (Gen.18.1–15). A promise is made to the patriarch here. Where do we find its fulfilment?
- Identify the links in the sequence of Gen.18–25 (character: Abraham).
- Note the 'sandwich' construction of Mark 3.20–35.

Mark's 'sandwiches'

In Mark 11.12–14, Jesus goes out with his disciples from Bethany and, seeing a fig tree without figs when he is hungry, declares that no one will ever eat its fruit. Immediately afterwards, the reader is led into the rough episode of the merchants driven from the temple (11.15–19). Then we return to the fig tree (11.20), which the disciples see is withered to the roots; this gives way to Jesus' teaching on prayer (11.21–26). To interrupt an episode and take it up again after an intermediate scene is to create a 'sandwich'.

Mark is fond of this procedure: 3.20–35 (inserted sequence, 3.22–30); 4.1–20 (vv.10–13); 5.21–43 (vv.25–34); 6.7–30 (vv.14–29); 11.12–21 (vv.15–19); 14.1–11 (vv.3–9); 14.17–31 (vv.22–26); 14.53–72 (vv.55–65); 15.20–16.8 (15.42–46).

This dovetailing of events is not just dramatically astute. The interlocking triggers off an echo between the scene inserted and the scene into which it is inserted, and this echo produces enhanced meaning: the two scenes interpret each other. We shall be emphasizing this interpretative interaction in the next chapter (> 4.4). In the case of the story of the fig tree, its sterility and the verdict of barrenness passed on it prepare metaphorically for Jesus' judgment on the temple, which is described as a 'den of thieves' (11.17b); the teaching to which it gives rise points to prayer, of which the temple has ceased to be the place (11.17a): 'Have faith in God. . .'(11.22).

For further reading
J. L. Ska, *'Our Fathers have Told Us'*, Subsidia Biblica 13, Rome: Pontifical Biblical Institute 1990, 1–3 (criteria for closures).

4

The plot

For there to be a narrative there has to be a story. The structure of the story is its *plot*. We have seen that the narrative differs from the description by virtue of four factors (> 1.5), the most important being the presence, in a narrative, of a plot. So here we are at the heart of what constitutes a narrative.

Our approach will be to begin by defining the plot (4.1), then two approaches to the plot will be suggested (4.2–3); then various combinations of plots will be considered (4.4–5) before a presentation of the two basic types, resolution plots and revelation plots (4.6).

4.1 The plot makes the narrative

'Now the famine was severe in Samaria' (I Kings 18.2b): if the narrator stops there, he is limiting himself to a description; he is not yet telling a story. But he goes on: 'Now the famine was severe in Samaria. And Ahab called Obadiah, who was over the household, and said to him, "Go through the land to all the springs of water and to all the valleys; perhaps we may find grass and save the horses and mules alive"' (I Kings 18.2b, 3,5). To go that far is already to tell a story, at any rate the beginning of a story.

The difference between the non-narrative and the narrative lies in the causal relationship constructed by the discourse. The narrator has established a connecting link between 'The famine was severe in Samaria' and 'Ahab called Obadiah'. This link can be contingent, probable or necessary – that doesn't

matter. Once a significant causal relationship is established between two facts, there is a narrative. The first narrator is the one who, bringing two facts together, has produced a hypothesis or a certainty relating to the link between the two.

What is called a plot

'Now the famine was severe in Samaria. And Ahab called Obadiah, who was over the household and said to him. . .' This narrative is evidently embryonic. The content is going to get more complex (as a result of the meeting with Elijah), but nevertheless it will keep this basic structure, which is to systematize a series of events.

This unifying structure which links the various happenings in the story and organizes them into a continuous account is called '*plot*'. The plot safeguards the unity of action and gives meaning to the multiple elements in the story. It is on this specific point that the narrative is distinct from the chronicle, which simply enumerates facts. The narrative does not just enumerate: changing the order of reality, by means of the plot it substitutes a causal order. Linked together by a causal logic, the facts are thus made necessary by the narrative.

Paul Ricoeur defines the plot as 'the set of combinations by which events are made into a story' (*From Text to Action*, 4). In a word, it is the plot that makes the narrative. It is through the plot that the reader perceives, in the series of related actions, something more than an accumulation of facts lined up in no particular order. The plot is the unifying

---

DEFINITIONS

Plot: systematization of the events which make up the story: these events are linked together by a causal link (configuration) and inserted into a chronological process (sequence of events).

---

principle of the narrative, its scarlet thread: it makes it possible to organize the stages of the story into a coherent scenario.

A question immediately arises: what narrative closure does one adopt to determine the plot? Must one consider the micro-narrative or the global narrative (a Gospel, for example). We shall begin from the smallest unit, the micro-narrative (the episode), before moving to broader narrative surfaces.

The organization of the plot corresponds to a logic which can be described in a narrative grammar. Aristotle already laid the foundations for this when he defined the plot (*muthos*) as 'the arrange-

ment of the incidents' (*Poetics* 1450a, 8 and 12). What grammar governs this system?

The classical plot

In his treatise on *Poetics*, Aristotle observes and comments on the plot in tragedy. According to him a drama is constructed with two sides, the complication and the denouement: 'In every tragedy there is a complication and a denouement. The incidents outside the plot and some of those in it usually form the complication, the rest is the denouement. I mean this, that the complication is the part from the

PYRAMID PLOT

41

EXPOSITION   COMPLICATION   TRANSFORMING ACTION

beginning up to the part which immediately precedes the occurrence of a change from bad to good fortune or from good fortune to bad: the denouement is from the beginning of the change down to the end' (1455b, 24–29). Aristotle thus sees the plot articulated around a reversal which tips the destiny of the hero towards happiness or misfortune.

We need to remember the pyramid structure of this classical approach to the plot. At the base, there is an obstacle to cross or a difficulty to resolve. At the apex, there is the transforming action which brings a move from the perception of a difficulty (the complication) to its resolution (the denouement). The plot pivots around a move towards action, which is prepared for by the preceding narrative and the end of which it expounds.

The labels by which critics designate these three constitutive moments differ: I. complication; II. reversal or climax; III. denouement or resolution.

Here, by way of example, is Luke 4.40:

WHAT THEY HAVE SAID ABOUT THE PLOT

'The plot, as a chain of facts, is based on the presence of an internal tension between these facts which has to be created at the beginning of the story, maintained during its development and which must find its resolution in the denouement' (R. Bourneuf and R. Quellet, *L'Univers du roman*, Paris: Pressses Universitaires de France 1972, 43).

'The plot in a dramatic or narrative work is constituted by its events and actions, as they are rendered and ordered toward achieving particular emotional and artistic effects. This description is deceptively simple, because the actions (including verbal discourse as well as physical actions) are performed by particularly characters in a work, and are the means by which they exhibit their moral and dispositional qualities. Plot and character are therefore independent critical concepts' (M. H. Abrams, *A Glossary of Literary Terms*, Chicago: Holt Rinehart and Winston 1988, 159).

'At the beginning everything is possible; in the middle things become probable; at the end everything is necessary' (P. Goodman, *The Structure of Literature*, Chicago: University of Chicago Press 1954, 14).

DÉNOUEMENT   FINAL SITUATION

'1. Now when the sun was setting, all those who had any that were sick with various diseases brought them to him; 2. and he laid his hands on every one of them 3. and healed them.'

4.2 The quinary scheme

P. Larivaille ('L'analyse (morpho)logique du récit') must be given the credit for having refined the Aristotelian model; for Aristotle, while positing the need for unity of action around the reversal, did not describe its function. On the basis of an analysis of folk tales, Larivaille noted that the reversal produced by the central action brings about a transition from a universe which is troubled (by a desire, a sickness, a shortage) to a universe which is re-established. The classic case is the story of a miracle which begins with a state of sickness and ends with someone who has been healed. The action on which the narrative pivots can thus be called transforming, to the degree that it transforms a troubled initial state to a peaceful final state.

From this perspective, every narrative is defined by the presence of two narrative markers (initial situation and final situation), between which a relationship of transformation is established. The transformation brings the subject from one state to the other, but this transition has to be triggered off (complication) and applied (denouement). Hence the *quinary* scheme (its name comes from the figure 5 in Latin); this scheme brings to five the number of stages of which the plot is typically made up.

1. Initial situation (or exposition)
2. Complication
3. Transforming action
4. Denouement
5. Final situation

This scheme has become established as the canonical model by which any plot can be measured.

An application: Matthew 8.14–15

The little story of the healing of Peter's mother-in-law (Matt.8.14–15) precisely embodies the five stages of the quinary scheme.

The **initial situation** (or **exposition**) gives the readers the pieces of information necessary to understand the situation that the story is to change. This exposition specifies the who, what and (sometimes) how.

'When Jesus went into Peter's house' (8.14): the initial situation is constituted by Jesus' arrival at Peter's house: this brings Jesus into contact with what happens in the disciple's house.

The **complication** (or **knot**) triggers off the action. It is here that the dramatic tension usually begins. The detonator can be the statement of a difficulty, a conflict, an incident, a hindrance in the way of the resolution of a problem.

'He saw his mother-in-law lying sick with a fever' (8.14b): Jesus' entrance is made problematical by the presence in the house of a sick woman whom he sees. Two parameters are specified: the state of the sick person (lying down with a fever) and her social proximity to Peter (mother-in-law).

The **transforming action** aims at removing the difficulty or the shortage or the disturbance announced by the story. The transforming dynamic can consist of a particular action or a long process of change. Classically, the turning point of the story is situated here.

'He touched her hand and the fever left her' (8.15a). The therapeutic gesture and its effect correspond to the confrontation of Jesus with the situation of the sickness. This confrontation is trans-formed by the expulsion of the fever, which leaves the woman and then leaves the place where Jesus is.

The **denouement** is a stage symmetrical with the complication. It states the resolution of the problem indicated. It describes the effects of the transforming action on the people concerned or the way in which the situation is re-established in its former state.

'She arose' (8.15b): the situation of lying is matched by a rising. The woman moves from fragility to strength, from being an object (dependent) to being a subject (capable of movement).

The **final situation** sets out the recognition of the new state (after the elimination of the difficulty) or the return to normality (after the disappearance of the disturbance). This stage, which Greek tragedy called *katastrophe*, describes the new situation after the narrative tension set up by the narrative has been relaxed.

'And she served them' (8.15b): the final situation is surprising, but it corresponds to the initial state (Jesus comes into the house). The handicap which appeared between the woman and the master has been removed by an act of healing. Information about the condition of the Jewish woman in first-century Palestine surprises the modern reader:

DEFINITIONS

Quinary scheme: a structural model splitting up the plot of the narrative into five successive moments:

1. **Initial situation** (or **exposition**): the circumstances of the action (setting, characters), if need be a shortage of something is indicated (sickness, difficulty, ignorance); the narrative will show an attempt to remove it.

2. **Complication:** an element that sets off the narrative, introducing narrative tension (a lack of equilibrium in the initial state or complication in the quest).

3. **Transforming action:** the outcome of the quest, reversing the initial situation: the transforming action is either at a pragmatic (action) or a cognitive (evaluation) level.

4. **Denouement (or resolution):** removal of the tension by the application of the transforming action to the subject.

5. **Final situation:** statement of the new state attained by the subject following the transformation. Structurally this moment corresponds to the reversal of the initial situation by an elimination of the shortage.

	II Kings 4.1–7	Mark 12.13–17	
Initial situation	Now the wife of one of the sons of the prophets cried to Elisha, 'Your servant my husband is dead; and you know that your servant feared the Lord,	And they sent to him some of the Pharisees and some of the Herodians,	**Initial situation**
Complication	but the creditor has come to take my two children to be his slaves.' And Elisha said to her, 'What shall I do for you? Tell me; what have you in the house?' And she said, 'Your maidservant has nothing in the house, except a jar of oil.'	to entrap him in his talk. And they came and said to him, 'Teacher, we know that you are true and care for no man; for you do not regard the position of men, but truly teach the way of God. Is it lawful to pay taxes to Caesar or not? Should we pay them, or should we not?' But knowing their hypocrisy, he said to them, 'Why put me to the test?	**Complication**
Transforming action	Then he said, 'Go outside, borrow vessels of all your neighbours, empty vessels and not too few. Then go in, and shut the door upon yourself and your sons, and pour into all these vessels; and when one is full, set it aside.' So she went from him and shut the door upon herself and her sons; and as she poured they brought the vessels to her. When the vessels were full, she said to her son, 'Bring me another vessel.' And he said to her, 'There is not another.' Then the oil stopped flowing.	Bring me a coin and let me look at it.' And they brought one. And he said to them, 'Whose likeness and superscription is this?' They said to him, 'Caesar's.'	**Transforming action**
Denouement	She came and told the man of God, and he said, 'Go, sell the oil and pay your debts,	Jesus said to them, 'Render to Caesar the things that are Caesar's and to God the things that are God's.'	**Denouement**
Final situation	and you and your sons can live on the rest.'	And they were amazed at him.	**Final situation**

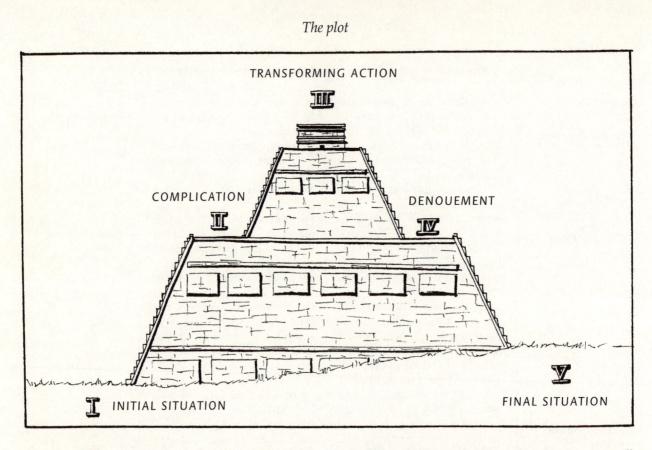

TRANSFORMING ACTION

III

COMPLICATION

II

DENOUEMENT

IV

I INITIAL SITUATION

V

FINAL SITUATION

women were forbidden to serve rabbis. The way in which Peter's mother-in-law serves bears witness to her cure and attests a freedom which makes her go well beyond the social conditions of the time.

How to identify a plot

There is no plot without a complication and a denouement; it is sometimes the identification of the complication which will begin the location of a plot. But most frequently, identifying the plot consists in discerning what the transforming action is.

Among the various actions or happenings which the story lines up, the transforming action is characterized by its decisive character; it works on the key issue of the story: the communication of an object (food, money, an animal, etc.) or an object-value (health, knowledge, power, peace. . .). But we need to be careful, since although the transforming action

is decisive, that does not mean that the narrator will put it at the centre of his narrative or that he will necessarily give it the longest description.

The dramatic tension of the narrative relates to the attainment of this object (-value) the attribution or non-attribution of which determines the good fortune or bad fortune of the person. To differentiate these two possible outcomes (good fortune and bad fortune), some scholars speak of a 'comic'-type resolution as opposed to a 'tragic'-type resolution. The parable about being watchful (Luke 12.42–28) alternates the one with the other, setting the condemnation of the unfaithful servant against the gratification of the first servant.

The stages of the plot either side of the transforming action correspond symmetrically.

The initial situation and the final situation correspond in a reverse form: the final state corresponds to the transformed state. A classical case of this is the healing story, where the state of being sick (stage 1) gives place to being healed (stage 5).

An analogous symmetry links the complication (stage 2) and the denouement (stage 4), since the first introduces a disturbing factor while the second arranges the resolution.

The indispensable and the optional

The innumerable variety of narratives teaches us one thing: the quinary scheme is implemented in very different ways depending on the narratives. The art of narration consists specifically in renewing *ad infinitum* the fashioning of the plot, even if for biblical narration we must reckon with a much greater stability of narrative forms than in the modern novel.

What are the elements needed to construct a plot and those that a narrative can pass over?

Beyond question the *transforming action* must be present, although it can be evoked without being described (one example is Psalm 22, where the

---

THE GOOD USE OF MODELS

IF NARRATION WERE A PROCESS OF NARRATIVE CLONING...

Let's specify once for all what can be expected of a model like the quinary scheme. The identification of a type of structure which can function as a generative model does not imply that all stories of all times can be reduced to this skeleton. If narration were a process of narrative cloning, it would only produce enormous boredom. The infinite variety of stories is there to prove the opposite.

What use is a model?

The structural model isn't a straitjacket. It's a scale against which stories can be measured to determine what is unique about them. The scale functions like the cabinet-maker's ruler (and not all his pieces of furniture are one metre long). It allows us: 1. To evaluate the originality of the story in comparison with the model, in particular through its way of emphasizing one element in the model to the detriment of another; 2. To grasp the effect sought by the narrator, who outsmarts the expectations of the readers by not offering or by holding back what the story leads them to expect.

change is indicated at v.22b with an enigmatic 'you have responded to me'). As we have said, the *complication* which triggers off the action is also necessary; without it there is no narrative.

The *initial situation* can be evoked surreptitiously. Three verses are enough to tell the reader of I Sam.8–10 about Samuel's old age and the perversion of his sons (8.1–3); on the other hand, the reluctance of Samuel to give the people a king and the circumstances of the anointing of Saul are told at length.

The narrator can leave out the *denouement* or the *final solution*, but not both. The absence of the final state is a recognized narrative procedure: the interrupted narrative. This trick of narrative suspension leads the reader to imply it for himself, imagining how the narrative would conclude.

Looking for the peak

Where does the plot reach its peak? That's a difficult question, since a distinction must be made between the pivot of the plot and the notion of dramatic tension. This must not be confused with the narrative tension which we have said is an essential part of the complication. While narrative tension triggers off the story (complication), the dramatic tension does not have a place assigned to it in the plot and corresponds to an emotional or pragmatic intensity,

Let's begin with the pivot: it is the turning point of the plot. It is the moment when things turn: the wise man replies to the question he is asked, the healer performs the therapeutic act, the traitor hands over his master. Normally this pivot coincides with the transforming action. Normally, too, this turning point coincides with the peak of the dramatic tension, before the story begins its descent

---

THE INTERRUPTED STORY

The parable of the workers at the eleventh hour (Matt.20.1–16) is a classic case of an interrupted story. When the workers engaged at dawn grumble about not having received more than those engaged at the last hour, the master replies: 'Am I not allowed to do what I will with my own? Is your eye evil because I am good?' (20.15). The story ends there. But what will be the reaction of the protesters? Will they accept the strange justice of the master? Or will they leave annoyed? Readers have to imagine an ending… in which they will express their own attitude to this questioning of retributive justice.

The procedure of narrative suspension appears here and there in the Hebrew Bible. The story of Jacob's marriage (Gen.29.1–30) ends with his being deceived with Leah; how will the emotional conflict end? The story of Jephthah (Judg.11.29–40) ends without the narration of the sacrifice of his daughter, promised by a vow (how did this take place?). II Kings concludes with the liberation of the exiled king of Judah, Jehoiakin (25.27–30); but what will

become of the people and their hoped-for return from exile? The Song of Songs ends on expectations (but how will the relationship continue?).

Within the New Testament the most spectacular case of an open ending is the Gospel of Mark, which in its original version ends with the fear of the women when confronted with the empty tomb (16.8; vv.9–20 were added in the second century to complete this abrupt ending). The evangelist Luke is the specialist in narrative suspensions: see the parable of the two sons in Luke 15.11–32 (will the older son join the feast?), the narrative of the temptations of Jesus in 4.1–13 (when will Satan withdraw?), the story of the woman who was a sinner at the home of Simon the Pharisee in 7.36–50 (will Simon be convinced?) or again the end of the book of Acts, 28.30–31 (will Paul appear before the emperor?).

For further reading

J. L. Magness, *Sense and Absence*, Atlanta: Scholars Press 1986 (narrative suspension in the Bible and particularly in Mark 16.8).

with the stage of the denouement: the sick person is healed, the traitor is discovered, the king regains his throne. In Greek tragedy, this is the moment when the hero has attained the apogee of his destiny (his 'fortune'). In the biblical story this is the moment when the character is decisively confronted with divine intervention.

However, we must not conclude from this that on either side of the transforming action the two parts of the story are necessarily of equal length. A mere glance at the text will make it possible to draw a diagram of the dramatic tension and to identify the peak(s). It is necessary to guard against giving the turning point a preconceived location. The pivot is not necessarily at the geometrical centre of the narrative. In the narrative of the encounter between the Risen Christ and Mary of Magdala (John 20.11–18), the complication is emphasized by the repetition of the question 'Woman, why are you weeping?', once by the angels (v.13) and a second time by Jesus (v.15). The pivot comes later, in v.16, when Mary recognizes the risen Christ.

Furthermore the pivot and the dramatic tension do not always coincide. In the same narrative in John 20, the tension mounts at the complication (misunderstanding prevails in vv.13–15) and takes a new turn immediately after the pivot with the Risen Christ's injunction, 'Do not touch me' (v.17). Here the dramatic tension is fixed around the pivot, on the one hand in the difficulty of recognizing the risen Christ and on the other in the withdrawal of Christ as soon as he is recognized.

4.3 An approach by modes

French semiotics, inspired by A. J. Greimas (*Sémantique structurale*), has developed another approach to the plot. First let us spell out the big difference in the levels on which narrative criticism and semiotics (or structural criticism) operate. Narrative criticism looks for the plot by following the movement of the story. Semiotics operates at a deeper level of abstraction, an infra-textual level; it is not interested in the geography of the story but in the formal structure to which it relates. That is why the semiotic approach to the plot works with a series of operations which will not necessarily all be presented by the story or necessarily in order.

This narrative grammar splits up the logical operations indispensable to the act of transformation into six stages.

The semiotic narrative programme

This narrative programme presents a scenario organized into six phases.

At the two extremes we find the initial situation and the final situation of the quinary scheme. The

---

Check your knowledge

- Establish the plot of the parable of the ten young women (Matt.25.1–13).
- Establish the plot of the story of the demolition of the altar of Baal (Judg 6.25–32).
- Where do you locate the dramatic tension and the pivot in the narrative of the healing of ten lepers (Luke 17.11–19)?

DEFINITIONS

Narrative tension: the element which triggers off the narrative (complication), corresponding in the plot to the moment of complication.

Dramatic tension: emotional or pragmatic intensity of the narrative, without any specific location within the plot.

Pivot: turning point in the plot, normally coinciding with the transforming action.

I **Initial situation** *Modes*	II **Manipulation** *ought to do* *want to do*	III **Competence** *know how to do* *be able to do*	IV **Performance** *do*	V **Sanction** *know*	VI **Final Situation**
Narrative programme	virtual	actual	realized	recognized	

performance corresponds to the transforming action: it brings about the attribution or acquisition of an object (value) by a subject. The originality of the scenario lies in the definition of phases II, III and V.

An application: I Kings 17.17–24
(the son of a widow of Zarephath)

I. Initial situation: an exposition of the circumstances of the action and a statement of the state of shortage.
The story of the raising of the son of a widow at Zarephath begins by stating the child's illness and his loss of breath (17.17b-18); this state of shortage constitutes the initial situation, the object-value to achieve being the child's life.

II. Manipulation: introduction of the operative subject (the author of the transforming action) in his mandate, bringing into play an ought to do and/or a want to do.
The prophet Elijah is asked to intervene by the woman (17.18). Her invective, 'What have I to do with you, man of God?', and her reproach, 'You have come to call to mind my sin and make my child die', are so many pressures on Elijah to act. Through the indignant intervention of the widow, Elijah arrives at a want to do: 'to restore life to the child'.

III. Competence: acquisition by the operative subject of the operational modes of be able to do and know how to do.
Elijah takes things in hand in the strict sense and in the metaphorical sense. He takes the child from the woman's arms and carries him up to the upper room. This whole passage describes in detail Elijah's know-how in taking care of the child (17.19b, 21–22). Elijah takes the side of the woman in invoking the Lord: does he want evil to befall this woman who has welcomed him by making her son die (17.20)? The address to the Lord and the threefold invocation of this Lord by Elijah (17.21) indicate that the origin of power has shifted: it is the Lord who will restore life to the child, having heard the voice of the prophet.

IV. Performance: action removing the shortage indicated in phase I.
17.22–23: Elijah takes the child and restores him to his mother. The miracle is noted. The child is alive and returns to his mother, but after the experience of a separation is a pledge of new relationships for her and for him.

V. Sanction: recognition of the new situation created: the sanction does not consist in noting the effect of the performance but in pronouncing on its value.
The woman, a foreigner, recognizes the prophet as a man of God and puts her trust in the Lord of whom he is the spokesman (17.24); the true origin of the healing has been identified.

Why modes are interesting

The two scenarios offered, one by the quinary scheme, the other by the semiotic narrative programme, do not claim to be compatible. As we have

The healing of the centurion's servant (Luke 7.1–10)

Quinary scheme		Semiotic narrative programme
Initial situation	When Jesus had ended all his sayings he entered Capernaum. Now a centurion had a slave who was dear to him, who was sick and at the point of death.	**Initial situation**
Complication	When he heard of Jesus, he sent to him elders of the Jews, asking him to come and heal his slave. And when they came to Jesus, they besought him earnestly saying, 'He is worthy to have you do this for him, for he loves our nation, and he built us our synagogue.'	**Manipulation (statement of ought to do)**
Transforming action	And Jesus went with them. When he was not far from the house, the centurion sent friends to him, saying to him, 'Lord, do not trouble yourself, for I am not worthy to have you come under my roof; therefore I did not presume to come to you. But say the word, and let my servant be healed. For I am a man under authority, with soldiers under me; and I say to one, "Go," and he goes, and to another, "Come," and he comes: and to my slave, "Do this," and he does it.'	**Competence (statement of able to do)**
Denouement	When Jesus heard this he marvelled at him, and turned and said to the multitude that followed him, 'I tell you, not even in Israel have I found such faith.'	**Sanction**
Final situation	And when those who had been sent returned to the house they found the slave well.	**Statement of the finished performance**

The quinary scheme reads the narrative as an attainment of faith by the centurion, while the semiotic narrative programme is attached to the performance of the healing (which is not related).

said, they work on different levels. The first draws up a geographical map of the story with the aid of a typical plan of the plot. The second model operates at an infra-textual level, reconstructing the logical mechanism of the narrative transformation with the help of an abstract category (the modes).

The quinary scheme formalizes the unfolding of the narrative, while the narrative programme presents more of an algorithm, i.e. a formula which recapitulates the elements needed for any narrative transformation. In fact the semiotic questioning takes place at a structural level which is not related to the chronology of the narrative.

We must repeat that there is no question of super-imposing the two approaches. But we should note the attention paid to modes. It is interesting to ask what registers the story uses: is the disturbing effect (the complication) a matter of ought to do or want to do, or of know to do or be able to do? Who mandates whom and for what? Who seeks power from whom? Who must trigger whose will?

Similarly, between the stage of complication and the final situation the formulation of Greimas' narrative programme helps us to unpack what relates to the effect of the transforming action (a statement), what relates to the final state (a statement), and what relates to the evaluation of this new state (value judgment).

4.4 The combination of plots

From a structural point of view, the narrative with a single plot and a pyramidal structure (complication – transforming action – denouement) is a pure form. Most frequently, the composition of plots lends itself to numerous combinations of which the biblical narrators make use: linked, overlapping, inserted or interlaced plots.

Linked plots

The parable of the talents (Matt.25.14–30) sets out an initial situation (vv.14–15). A landowner goes away, sharing his goods unequally between his three servants: two increase what they are given and the third buries it (vv.16–18).

At the moment of the transforming action, the narrative repeats the procedure of settling accounts, which sees the servants appearing on their master's return. The first servant is gratified by a happy denouement: 'Well done, good and faithful servant, you have been faithful in few things, so I shall set you over many: enter into the joy of your master' (v.21). The appearance of the second servant takes place in identical terms, and this arouses the reader's curiosity on the approach of the third appearance. This ends up with a tragic denouement: the third servant sees taken away from him the little that he has received (v.28) and thrown into infernal darkness (v.30: final situation).

On the basis of an identical beginning, the transforming action has unfolded three times; by this effect of repetition it has increased the dramatic tension about the fate of the third servant and the terrible verdict that is passed on him.

The chain repetition of a stage in the plot thus creates an effect of habit, which brings out all the more vividly the anomaly of the third repetition. That is the case in the parable of the talents. Elsewhere the effect of repetition operates by addition: the four announcements of Job's ruin (Job 1.13–19) or the six repetitions of Abraham's request about Sodom (Gen.18.16–33). It can also work by symmetrical opposition: the tragic annihilation of Ananias and Sapphira is a counter-model after the positive example of Barnabas (Acts 4.36–37), who sells his property and gives the price he gets for it to the community.

Whether by accumulation, addition or opposition, the linking of plots has the effect of repetition: the narrator constructs this effect with a view to making the narrative tension mount, leading either to a reinforcement or to a theatrical effect.

Overlapping

The last stage of a plot can form the start of the next.

Look at the way in which I Kings 18 and 19 follow

on: are Jezebel's threats against the prophet Elijah (I Kings 19.1–2) the final situation of the episode of the sacrifice on Carmel (I Kings 18)? Aren't they rather the initial situation of the episode of Elijah in the desert (I Kings 19)? In fact they are both. The ending of the first episode triggers off the next; that is why it is sometimes so difficult to trace the closure between two stories.

This process of overlapping, welding two plots together, gives a new twist to the action in order to surprise the reader.

Insertion

The evangelist Mark is the champion of inserting plots, which is also known as the 'sandwich' (> 3.5).

The story of the raising of Jairus' daughter (Mark 5) begins with the father coming to Jesus and asking for the master to come and lay hands on her (5.21–23). Jesus complies with the request and goes with him, followed by a large crowd (v.24). The complication is brought about by someone from Jairus' house saying, 'Your daughter is dead, why trouble the master further?' (v.35).

In the meantime another episode has taken place, with its own plot (v.25–34): a woman who has been afflicted with a loss of blood for twelve years has come up to Jesus on the way, touched him and has been cured, and when the Lord asks her questions she has thrown herself at his feet to tell him 'the whole truth'. But from v.35 on the plot of the first narrative resumes with the arrival of the people from Jairus' house; it continues with the arrival of the group at the home of the leader of the synagogue, the revival of the girl ('Little girl, I tell you, awake'), and Jesus' command to keep silent about this miracle.

The interlocking of the two stories, the one inserted into the other, makes them resonate. There is no lack of parallels. Both stories are about a woman. In both cases the figure twelve is mentioned: it is the duration of the woman's sickness and the age of the little girl. On both sides the suffering is dramatized: the gravity of the haemorrhage is emphasized and the death of the girl is announced. On both sides there is a prominent dualism between public and private, but in a reverse order: the woman has to move from a secret

MARK 5.21–43 IN NINE SCENES: LOOK FOR THE SANDWICH...

to a public confession (vv.30–33), while with Jairus Jesus passes from public to private (vv.40–43).

Beyond these likenesses, which a narrator could bring out by the simple addition of plots, what is the effect sought by this procedure of insertion? To see this, we have to note the precise point at which the story of Jairus works on the inserted story. After the people sent from his house have told Jairus of the death of his daughter, Jesus retorts to Jairus: 'Have no fear, only believe' (v.36). What kind of faith is this? And what credit is to be given to this request not to fear? The reader has just heard the reply to these questions: the faith is that shown by the woman with a flow of blood which Jesus has just sanctioned ('My daughter, your faith has saved you,' v.34). The call not to be afraid finds its credibility in the healing miracle which the woman has just experienced.

In other words, it is by a transfer of information from vv.25–34 that the reader grasps the relevance of the appeal made to Jairus by Jesus (v.36). But it has to be noted that this interlocking effect is orchestrated for the benefit of the reader. It is useless to ask whether Jairus was present at the intervening scene (partially in hiding!) between Jesus and the woman; besides, the narrator does not

indicate his presence between verses 25 and 34. The procedure of insertion is the instrument of a narrative strategy of which the reader is the target; the integration of one episode within a wider story is aimed at allowing a migration of information from the inserted story to the story into which it is inserted. Here it is the story into which another is inserted which requires the implantation of this narrative graft to be understood.

One could ask in what direction the information circulates from one plot to another in the other cases of Marcan 'sandwiches' listed above (> 3.5). In the case of the fig tree and the temple (Mark 11.12–25) it is manifestly the plot (the fig tree) into which the insertion is made which helps us to understand the inserted story (the temple).

Interlaced plots

The narrator can create a new narrative by mixing several plots.

One example is the story of Korah's rebellion, which interlaces three narratives about challenges to Moses and Aaron: Korah's rebellion against Aaron (Num.16.1a, 6–11, 16–24a, 27a, 35), the rebellion of the 250 elders of the community (Num. 16.2–5), and the rebellion of Dathan and Abiram against Moses (Num.16.1b, 12–15, 24b–34). Historical tradition classically divides these three stories into different traditions. When we read the story narratively as presented to us (cf. Ps.106.16–18; Sirach 45.18), we see that the combination of plots increases the complexity and the virulence of the conflict. The opposition to Moses, who according to Dathan and Abiram is leading his people to their death in the wilderness, is paralleled by a challenge to Aaron as priest on the part of Korah and his supporters and a challenge from the 250 elders. The ordeal decides between Moses and the supporters of Korah and the 250 opponents; Dathan and Abiram are swallowed up in Sheol (16.31–35). The story ends with a sign to remind the people: Korah's censers serve as a covering for the altar. However, the plot takes on a further twist with a rebellion of

---

Check your knowledge

- Linked plots: note the effect of linking in the sequences of the ten plagues of Egypt (Ex.7.8–11.10). How is Pharaoh's attitude presented to the reader?
- Overlapping: what particular position does the scene of the ascension occupy in Luke's work (Luke 24 and Acts 1)?
- Inserted plots: the book of Revelation is constructed round great sequences called 'sevens': the seven letters to the churches (2–3), the seven seals (6.1–8.1), the seven trumpets (8.6–11.19), the seven cups (16). Note the alternation which arises, just before these sevens, between the 'heavenly' and 'earthly' scenes.

the people, to which the Lord responds with a general pestilence. But the liturgical act of absolution for the people performed by Aaron rehabilitates him in his priestly functions (Num.17.12–13). His staff, the only one to blossom, seals the privilege of his tribe and his specific role.

The mixed sequences

The narrator can also mix the genres and compose mixed sequences in which narratives and discourse alternate. This alternation of narrative and discourse is typical of the book of Numbers, the Fourth Gospel and the Acts of the Apostles.

Here is an example taken from Acts: 2.42–5.42, in which the narrator describes the life of the Christian community in Jerusalem after Pentecost. This sequence is built on a carefully balanced alternation of summaries (brief narrative résumés), episodes and discourses. The succession is well orchestrated: a summary (2.42–47), an episode (3.1–11), a discourse (3.12–16), an episode (4.1–7), a discourse (4.8–12), an episode (4.13–22), an episode (4.23–31), a summary (4.32–35), an episode (4.36–37), an episode (5.1–11), a summary (5.12–16), an episode (5.17–26), a discourse (5.37–40), a summary (5.41–42). The signification here is constructed by the interaction of the different genres. The summaries state synthetically the state of the community's communion: the episodes specify this state of communion and expose the community to the hostility of the Sanhedrin; the discourses unfold to the crowd and the Sanhedrin the meaning of the events narrated by the episodes. The heterogeneity of the narrative fabric between Acts 2.42 and 5.42 is the instrument of a refined didactic aim.

4.5 Unifying plot and episodic plot

Each narrative episode (or micro-narrative) takes place in a narrative chain which can be broken up into segments (the sequence: > 3.5) or considered in its entirety (the macro-narrative). To this point the plot has been envisaged at the level of the micro-narrative. Now the broader narrative complexes constructed by the narrator (sequence and macro-narrative) have their own plot which encompasses and overhangs the plot of the smaller units. So we need to differentiate between an episodic plot (micro-narrative) and a unifying plot (sequence or macro-narrative). It is worth paying attention to this, since the integration of the micro-narrative into its context is extremely revealing about the course of the reading which the narrator means to suggest to his readers.

We saw above (>4.3) how the episodic plot of Luke 7.1–10 (the healing of the centurion's son) focussed on the mobilization of Jesus' power. Similarly, we could see that the episodic plot of Luke 7.36–50 (Jesus and the woman who was a sinner in the home of Simon the Pharisee) is fixed on the recognition of forgiveness as liberating grace. Now these two episodes are brought together in a

EPISODIC PLOT

DEFINITIONS

Episodic plot: a plot the narrative markers of which coincide with the micro-narrative.

Unifying plot: the plot of a narrative sequence or macro-narrative which overhangs and encompasses the plots of the episodes which it contains.

Resolution plot: a plot the transforming action of which operates at the pragmatic level (exploit, healing, etc.)

Revelation plot: a plot the transforming action of which consists in a gain of knowledge about a character in the story.

---

sequence which takes the reader from 7.1 to 7.50; the theme of this sequence is the recognition of the prophetic authority of Jesus, since the narrator constantly returns to it (vv.16, 28 and 39); moreover the raising of a widow's son at Nain (7.11–17) reminds the reader of another healing of a widow's son by a prophet (Elijah at Zarepath, I Kings 17.17–24; for this procedure of implicit commentary see > 8.2). The result is that these two episodic plots fall within the unifying plot of Luke 7 (recognizing Jesus as prophet), this being overhung by the unifying plot of the Gospel (recognizing Jesus as Christ).

4.6 Resolution plot, revelation plot

If in the sequence of Luke 7 the issue in the unifying plot is the recognition of Jesus as prophet, that signifies that the object-value (> 4.3 and 5.3) around which this plot turns is not in the order of doing but in that of knowing. The plot is a so-called *revelation* plot, since it culminates in a gain in knowledge. When the transforming action essentially involves a doing, and thus is situated at a pragmatic level (a request for healing, a search of purity, a desire for an encounter), it is called a *resolution* plot. Thus the episodic plot of Luke 7.1–10 is of a resolution type, while the unifying plot of Luke 7 and that of the macro-narrative, the Gospel, are of a revelation type.

It will be objected that every quest of the hero moves in both these registers, the pragmatic and the cognitive, at the same time: to acquire a good it is necessary to be able to do (pragmatic) and know

how to do (cognitive). But in a resolution plot the knowledge is put at the service of the acquisition of a good; in the case of a revelation plot the opposite is the case: the doing becomes the instrument of an increase in knowledge.

When the evangelist John develops the discourses after the narratives about actions, he excels in passing from the pragmatic to the cognitive level. To see this compare John 5.1–9a (the healing at Bethzatha) and the discourse which follows (9b-47), or John 9.1–7 and the dialogue in vv.8–41. This procedure is an indication that, unlike the Synoptics, in the Fourth Gospel the issue in the healing narratives is to be found in the recognition of the identity of the healer.

In the setting of the Synoptic tradition the evangelists do not treat the narratives identically. The parable of the talents is told with a resolution plot in Matt.25.14–30 (the issue is the performance of the servants and their gratification) but with a revelation plot in Luke 19.11–28 (the identity of the royal claimant is at issue).

Check your knowledge

- Is the plot of Exodus 17.1–17 (Massah and Meribah) a resolution or a revelation plot?
- Establish the plot of Luke 10.29–37 (the Good Samaritan) and of 10.38–42 (Martha and Mary). How do these episodic plots fit into the unifying plot of Luke 10.25–42?

The plot

RESOLUTION PLOT

REVELATION PLOT

For further reading

S. Bar-Efrat, *Narrative Art in the Bible*, JSOTS 70, Sheffield Academic Press 1988, 47–92 (plots in the Old Testament narration).

P. Ricoeur, *Time and Narrative I*, Chicago: University of Chicago Press 1990, 7–28 (the notion of plot).

J. L. Ska, *'Our Fathers Have Told Us'*, Subsidia Biblica 13, Rome: Pontificio Istituto Biblico 1990, 17–38 (types of plot in biblical narration).

5

The characters

The plot functions like the frame of an umbrella: it holds the whole thing together. However, the frame is not what someone looking at an umbrella sees first; that is the fabric, which makes the umbrella attractive and colourful. Both the fabric and the frame are indispensable (try going out with an umbrella reduced to the frame!), but the former is always more visible than the latter. Now that we have explored the hidden frame of the narrative, its plot, we move on to a more manifest dimension: the characters. Besides, isn't a story usually referred to by the name of its hero or heroine?

It will be clear that the metaphor of the umbrella can be pushed too far. Plot and characters cannot be separated; they belong together so closely that if we develop the one we shift the others. The characters are the visible face of the plot: they get it moving, they feed it, they dress it up; without them the plot is reduced to a skeleton. Conversely, a handful of characters does not make up a narrative until a plot connects them together.

5.1 The characters bring the story to life

To begin with, let's be a bit methodical. How do we classify characters? Must we begin from a system of values (the good and the bad), or their states of mind, their importance, their role in the plot?

Practices have changed over the course of history. With Aristotle, things are clear: the characters almost always fit into two categories, vice and virtue. The philosopher says that writers represent 'the active characters, who must necessarily be either heroic or inferior. . . It is just in this respect that tragedy differs from comedy. The latter sets out to represent people as worse than they are today, the former as better' (*Poetics* 1448a, 1–2, 15–17). Here we already have the notion of identification suggested to the reader; we shall be returning to this later (>5.5). We need to keep in mind that, for Aristotle, the most important thing about the role of characters is that they guide the action: the type of conduct (good fortune or bad fortune) will determine the genre of the narrative.

From the end of the Middle Ages, and even more with the appearance of the modern novel in the

A PLOT WITHOUT CHARACTERS

eighteenth century, the portrayal of the character gains in psychological depth: the approach to the character's personality is considerably refined. It is not until the school of Russian formalists at the beginning of the twentieth century, with Vladimir Propp, that we return to a view of the characters centred more on their function than on the features of their character. In his book *Morphology of the Folktale* (1928), Propp listed the major characters typical of the Russian magic story. His classification covers seven spheres of action: the aggressor, the giver, the princess and her father, the mandator, the hero, the false hero, the helper. French semiotics followed him but simplified the scheme (see 5.3). Generally speaking, it can be said that French structuralists and semioticians see the characters in the story as *agents* playing a role in the development of the story.

The American narratologists, led by Seymour Chatman, adopt a different perspective. They regard the characters as autonomous beings; they are interested in their characters' traits, their personality. According to Chatman, if a theory of characters is to be valid it must preserve at least two things: 1. an openness; 2. character traits which we recognize in autonomous beings. In other words, the characters in a story have open personalities, subject to change, to enrichment, to revision, and one is engaged in observing the course of the character constructed by the narrative (*Story and Discourse*, 119).

We shall not choose between these two approaches, as we are interested in a combination of them. First we shall present the semiotic theory of actants (5.3), before touching on the question of the autonomy of characters and studying more precisely the relationship which becomes established between reader and characters (identification, evaluation, position of the reader: 5.4–8).

However, we should not leave Aristotle too soon; first we must appreciate how right his intuition was. An approach of a formalist type, which tends to classify characters by virtue of their role in the plot, cannot fail to pay attention (in a way which can be called discursive) to the system of values which motivates these characters. Take, for example, the exorcism of the demoniac in Mark 5.1–20: it is interesting to group in the category of 'opponents' both the demons who have taken possession of the man and the crowd which begs Jesus to go away; but at the same time it is necessary to specify the different value-systems embodied by these figures.

THE CHARACTER, INDISPENSABLE AND TASTY

'Thought and character are the natural causes of any action and it is in virtue of these that all men succeed or fail – it follows then that it is the plot which represents the action. By "plot" I mean here the arrangement of the incidents: "character" is that which determines the quality of the agents, and "thought" appears wherever in the dialogue they put forward an argument or deliver an opinion' (Aristotle, *Poetics* 1450a, 1–7).

'Thus the character is a product of combinations: the combination is relatively stable... and more or less complex (involving more or less congruent, more or less contradictory focus); this complexity determines the character's "personality", which is just as much a combination as the odour of a dish or the bouquet of a wine' (R.Barthes, *S/Z*, 1990, 67).

'There is a story only if there are both events and existents [= characters]. There cannot be events without existents. And although it is true that a text can contain existents without events (a portrait, a descriptive essay), no one would dream of calling it a narrative' (S.Chatman, *Story and Discourse*, 1978, 113).

5.2 Classifying the characters

There are three possible types of classification, depending on whether one takes into account the number of characters, the intensity of their presence or their constitutive features.

Number is no problem: the people in the story can appear sometimes in the singular and sometimes as a collective (viz., the disciples).

The degree to which a character is present is already more tricky to determine, for the narrative itself generates, more or less distinctly, a hierarchy of major roles, subordinate roles and walk-ons. Those with major roles are called *protagonists*. The protagonists play an active role in the plot and are in the foreground. They include the hero who comes as a saviour, the king who sets his army on the march, the sick person who goes in search of a healer. In complete contrast to the protagonists, the walk-ons remain in the background; they can be individuals or collectives: a crowd, an inhabitant, a passer-by. Between these two extremes (protagonists and walk-ons) are the subordinate roles, which can be called *agents*. Their function is limited to helping the plot along; they can have a symbolic dimension.

Who is the agent in the story of the healing of a possessed child in Luke 9.37–43? The protagonists are obvious: Jesus, the father of the child, his son, the demon who holds him captive. The background is the great crowd which comes to meet Jesus: only at the end of the story is it said that 'all were struck by the greatness of God'. The role of the agent is played by the disciples who could not drive away the unclean spirit; in fact they do not intervene but serve as a point of reference by emphasizing the inability of human beings to cope with this kind of distress.

Round and flat

The previous type of classification, connected with the degree to which a character is present, is tricky to manipulate (is the intensity of presence a quantitative or a qualitative criterion?). If one gives preference to the traits that determine a character, one is in a position to objectify the consistency of the narrative, and that allows a more subtle diagnosis. E.M.Forster (*Aspects of the Novel*, 73–80) has proposed a distinction between *flat characters* and *round characters*. Flat characters are reduced to a single trait: thus the Pharisees in the story about plucking ears of corn (Mark.2.23–28). In this micronarrative the Pharisees content themselves with making the well-known objection: 'Look at what they are doing on the sabbath! That is not allowed!' By contrast, in the following episode (Mark 3.1–6, a healing on the sabbath), the Pharisees take on more substance and become a round character (a collec-

---

DEFINITIONS

Character: an individual or collective figure in the narrative, assuming a role in the plot.

Protagonist: a simple or complex character, playing an important role in the development of the plot.

Walk-on: a simple character, playing a passive or quasi-passive (background) role in the narrative.

Agent: a simple character, playing a minor (or single) role in the development of the plot.

Round character: a character constructed by means of several traits: this character frequently assumes the role of protagonist in the narrative.

Flat character: a character with a single trait.

Block character: a character whose role is invariable throughout the narrative or macro-narrative.

FLAT CHARACTER   →   ←   ROUND CHARACTER

tive one): they watch Jesus to see if he will cure the man with a paralysed hand (v.2), they are silent after hearing the question addressed to them (v.4), they look for a reason for accusing Jesus (v.2), and end up making a plot with the Herodians about how to do away with Jesus (v.6).

A variant is the block character, who keeps an unvarying role throughout the narrative or macro-narrative. This is the case with the collective character of the 'Pharisees' in the Gospel of Matthew.

An application: II Kings 5

What classification of characters does the narrative of the healing of Naaman (II Kings 5.1–27) suggest? From the start we can distinguish three protagonists: Naaman, Elisha and Gehazi.

Naaman is a ruler, a valiant warrior (the text even says that he is the one to whom the Lord gave the victory over Aram). However, this strong man appears in all his vulnerability: he is a leper. Having heard of the prophet who is in Samaria, he asks his master to be allowed to go there. His mood is not improved by the rather rude welcome given to him by Elisha (who simply sends a messenger to give him instructions). At that moment Naaman is irritated and ready to go back. One of his servants has

to intervene to convince him to follow the prophet's orders. When he has been cured, after immersing himself seven times in the waters of the Jordan, this man undergoes a real 'conversion', recognizing that 'there is no God in all the earth but in Israel' (v.15). His concern is then to go to offer a present and obtain forgiveness for an act which he will be forced to perform, accompanying his master to the house of the god Rimmon. Naaman then does not hesitate to give to Gehazi more than Gehazi asks for. We are in the presence of a character who is both strong and frail, reticent then submissive, preoccupied with ordering his life by his new convictions. Naaman is a round character.

The prophet Elisha is also a round character. He intervenes four times. Knowing that the king of Israel reacted in despair when confronted by the request of the king of Aram, he presents himself as the one who will know how to respond to Naaman's expectations. His attitude to Naaman is curious: he does not deign to move, but sends a messenger to him. Elisha then appears as a prophet filled with a quite remarkable tolerance (v.19). On the other hand, towards Gehazi his attitude becomes that of a judge who condemns the crime. In turns remote or involved, conciliatory or intransigent, Elisha is constructed as a complex personality.

This cannot be said of Gehazi, his servant. The only feature which emerges from the description is his greed: seeking to profit from the situation, he envisages deriving material benefit from the healing of Naaman and uses a subterfuge to gain his purpose. Given the importance of his role in the new development in the plot in vv.20–27, Gehazi is a protagonist, but the story constructs him as a flat character, with just one trait.

The girl prisoner and Naaman's wife (vv.2–3) serve as agents: from the narrative point of view their rule is limited to ensuring the transmission of knowledge (there is a prophet in Samaria who can cure him of leprosy). The king of Aram and the king of Israel are other agents. The king of Aram is an authoritative character who is used to being obeyed (v.5). The king of Israel is completely overwhelmed by the request of the king of Aram, which seems to him to be exorbitant: he has the impression that the latter is looking for a quarrel (v.7).

As for Naaman's servants, the narrator moves them from the status of agents to that of walk-ons. In v.13 they play a decisive role in persuading their master to submit to the prophet's instructions in spite of everything: they are agents. On the other hand, at the end of the story (vv.23–24) the two servants of Naaman who accompany Gehazi are no more than walk-ons. Other walk-ons are the Syrians (v.2), Naaman's entourage (v.15), the two members of the group of prophets (v.22). Agents and walk-ons are flat characters, described by a single trait, but sometimes this single trait is enough to move the plot on.

We must note a last character who is not directly present in the story but is constantly in the background: God. He gives victory to Aram (v.1). He is the one with whom the king cannot identify (v.7). He is the one whom Elisha represents (v.11). It is his intervention through the prophet that Naaman is waiting for (v.11). He is discovered by this military leader (v.15) who from now on refuses to offer any sacrifice to another god (v.17). He is the one from whom Naaman awaits forgiveness (v.18). He is the one for whom Gehazi shows no respect (v.20). This presence is set over against that of the god of Aram, Rimmon, just as the Jordan is set over against the Abana and the Pharpar, the rivers of Damascus (v.12); this presence gives meaning to the whole narrative. But we can see that the narrative treatment is special: the object of constant but oblique reference, God is direct subject only in v.1; this character (in the narrative sense) remains in filigree, and only the readers will be able to identify him, if they will, as the true agent (or principal character) of the story.

Check your knowledge

- What hierarchy of characters does the narrative of the confrontation between David and Nathan present (II Sam.12.1–25)?
- How do you classify the characters (protagonists, walk-ons, agents) in the story in Luke 7.11–17, the resurrection of a young man at Nain?

5.3 The actantial scheme

Working on the intuitions of Vladimir Propp, A.J.Greimas has sought to simplify and universalize the seven great characters detected by the Russian formalist. He has succeeded in formalizing the typical roles in all stories in a scheme which links together six actantial positions. In the process Greimas invented a term, actant, to differentiate both the agent and the character (*Sémantique structurale*, 156f.).

What is an actant? An actant is the one who performs the function needed to bring about the transformation which is at the centre of the narrative (> 4.2). The scheme above lists the six actantial positions. The basic idea is that every story presents a Subject chasing after a valuable Object (health, wealth, knowledge, etc.). The Despatcher mobilizes the Subject for the quest of the Object, which he must give to the Receiver; to do this the Despatcher and the Subject are linked (explicitly or implicitly)

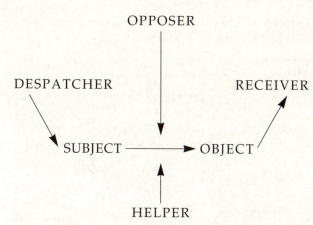

by contract. In the realization of the question the Subject can be helped (the Helper) or encounter obstacles (the Opposer).

The table below applies this grid to two texts, Charles Perrault's story of Cinderella and the story of the healing of the blind Bartimaeus (Mark 10.46–52).

It is necessary to assess the consequences of the choice of this neologism actant. It denotes a narrative function essential to the plot and nothing more. So it is important to remove from the idea of the character any psychological colouring and keep only its functional dimension: that is why Greimas resists using the words character or actor, which suggest a psychological depth in the agents, and above all betray the structuralist perspective while remaining down in the narrative. Now structuralism is interested in what governs the action in depth and takes place at a higher level of abstraction. The actantial position can therefore be filled by several characters in the story (Cinderella's stepmother and her daughters figure as the Opposer); the same character can accumulate several actantial posts (the fairy godmother is both the Despatcher and the Helper); an inanimate object or a feeling (the Prince's love) can also assume the role of actant.

A return to II Kings 5

The actantial scheme forms a good grid for reading the narrative of Elisha and Naaman (II Kings 5); it discloses an unexpected complexity in the construction of the narrative.

There is no need to hesitate much over the identity of the subject, Naaman. His quest consists in regaining health (the Object). But who is the Despatcher? Is it he himself or is it more precisely his desire to be healed? Is it not also the little captive who speaks to her mistress? Or could it be the king of Aram who sends a message to the king of Israel to put pressure on him? The point remains to be clarified. The Receiver is certainly Naaman himself. There are many Opposers: the king of Israel, disconcerted by this embarrassing official request, then Naaman's own doubts about Elisha's instructions to immerse himself in the Jordan. At this moment Naaman's servants certainly play the role of Helpers.

A key moment in the story is the offer of a present to Elisha (v.15), which the prophet refuses in the

	Cinderella	*Mark 10.46–52*
Subject:	Cinderella	Jesus
Object:	The prince's love	The healing
Despatcher	Her fairy godmother	God
Receiver	Cinderella + Prince	Bartimaeus
Helper	Her fairy godmother	The faith of the blind man
Opposer	Stepmother + her daughters	The crowd

DEFINITIONS

Descriptive pause: an extreme slowing down of the narration in which a segment of the narrative corresponds to zero duration at the level of the story.

Scene: so-called 'normal' rhythm of the narration, in which narrative and story conventionally go forward at the same pace (for example the dialogue).

Summary: acceleration of the narration in which the narrative relates succinctly a relative long period of the story.

Ellipse: extreme pace of the narration, which passes over a period of the story in silence: this temporal segment corresponds to a zero segment in the narrative.

John tells us nothing about this stay in Ephraim which he limits himself to mentioning. The next part of the narrative corresponds completely to this deliberate silence. During the next three verses (vv.55–57) there is nothing more about the actions of the protagonist: we learn that Passover was near, that many people were going up to Jerusalem, that the whole world was looking for Jesus, and that the high priests had given the order to seize him if he were discovered. Then at the beginning of chapter 12 we read: 'Six days before the Passover Jesus arrived in Bethany, . . .' On the narrative level the effect of John's silence on Jesus' stay in Ephraim is remarkable: it brings out the reaction of the crowds and the chief priests, and subtly pursues the story of Jesus, but at a deeper level (by absence).

Later, after the arrest of Jesus, we read in 18.24: 'Ananias then sent Jesus bound to Caiaphas, the high priest.' We have to wait until v.28 for the sequel: 'Then they led Jesus from the house of Caiaphas to the praetorium.' Between the two, in three verses (vv.25–27) John tells the reader about the denial by Simon Peter. There is no mention of Jesus. As the appearance before Caiaphas unfolds, the narrative presents a gap (> 9.2); the construction of the character by the narrator does not leave the reader completely without means of imagining its content, from 11.49–52. But the gap remains. As a result, by virtue of this narrative silence, the blow inflicted on Jesus by one of the high priest's guards (18.22) closes the discussion on the Jewish side. The scene then shifts to the Roman authorities.

In narrative criticism, the temporal ellipse is a marker of the orientation of the story, revealing the point of view which secretly shapes the plot.

Check your knowledge

- What is the function of the summary in Matt.8.16–17, put in the middle of the scenes of Matthew 8?
- Find the pauses in the narrative of the making of the covenant on Sinai (Ex.24). What force do they give the narrative?
- After relating the birth of Moses, the book of Exodus does not speak of his adolescence (Ex.2, see v.11). How are we to interpret this ellipse?

7.2 Order

The narrator's play with time is not limited to choosing the pace of the narrative. There is a second equation between the chronology of the story and the time of the narrative: synchrony and anachrony. A synchronous narrative keeps pace with the chronology of the story (beginning with the beginning and ending with the end). Anachrony arises the moment that the story makes a jump, whether backwards (towards the past) or forward (towards the future).

A flashback: 'All that happened so that what the Lord had said by the prophet might be fulfilled. . .' The reference to the scriptures is one of the classic cases of flashback in the Gospels: this reminder of the past is called *analepsis*.

ANALEPSIS

MANY YEARS LATER, THE YOUNG ALBERT WAS TO BECOME A GREAT SCIENTIST

PROLEPSIS

A jump forward: 'Jesus taught his disciples and said to them, "The Son of man will be delivered into the hands of men. . ."' In the Gospels the announcement of the passion and the resurrection is a classic case of anticipation; it is called a *prolepsis*.

Internal or external references

Analepsis and prolepsis are the two cases of anachrony, creating a discord between the order of the narrative (narrative discourse) and that of the story.

If the force of the anachrony is considerable and goes beyond the thresholds of the narrative, it is said to be *external* anachrony. If on the contrary it falls completely within the setting of the story it is said to be *internal*. An analepsis or prolepsis can be *mixed*, which means that it evokes a chain of events that in part leapfrogs one of the thresholds of the narrative (beginning or end).

So it can be said that the announcements of the passion and resurrection are internal prolepses; none of them goes beyond the setting of the Gospel narrative. On the other hand, the events related in the eschatological discourse of Jesus are integrated into a vast external prolepsis of considerable force and amplitude; this discourse meets Peter's request:

'Tell us when this will happen, and what will be the sign of your coming and of the end of the world' (Matt.24.3b).

As for analepses, the references in the Gospels to the prophetic writings evidently go beyond the opening threshold of the story: they are said to be external. Stephen's speech in Acts, which unfolds a panoramic reading of the history of Israel from Abraham on, is an impressive example of external analepsis (in the chronology of the story, it goes back seventeen or eighteen centuries).

The announcement of the resurrection of Jesus in the Gospel of Mark is a prolepsis of a mixed type. It is confirmed by the discovery of the empty tomb (Mark 16.1–4: internal effect), but the words of the young man in the tomb relate to a point outside the story, where the Risen Christ precedes the disciples into Galilee (16.7).

The function of anachronies

Anachronies can perform several functions. We shall distinguish anachronies strictly linked to the control of the narrative (functional anachronies) from anachronies with a semantic impact, i.e. which contribute towards constructing the meaning.

Among the anachronies of a functional type we

THE ANACHRONIES BETWEEN FORGETFULNESS AND IMPATIENCE

'When we are told a story which refers to a narrative time I (the time at which the narrated events occur, which may be two hours ago or one thousand years ago), both the narrator (in the first or third person) and the character can refer to something that happened prior to the time of the narrated events. Or they can hint at something that, at the time of these events, has yet to occur and that is anticipated. As Gérard Genette says, a flashback seems to make up for something the author has forgotten, whereas the flashforward is a manifestation of narrative impatience' (U.Eco, *Six Walks in the Fictional Woods*, 30).

'An anachrony can be in the past or the future, more or less distant from the "present" moment, i.e. the moment in the story where the narrative is interrupted to give room to it: we shall call this temporal distance the force of the anachrony. It can also itself cover a longer or shorter duration of the story: that is what we shall call its *amplitude*' (C.Genette, *Figures III*, 89).

might mention this analepsis created by the author of the Acts of the Apostles when he tells of the martyrdom of Stephen: 'But they cried out with a loud voice and stopped their ears and rushed together upon him. Then they cast him out of the city and stoned him; *and the witnesses laid down their garments at the feet of a young man named Saul*' (7.57–58). If the narrator goes back to make this detail more specific, it is because of the importance that the character Paul will have further on in the narrative: some verses later, the text will mention him again: 'And Saul was consenting to his death' (8.1). The analepsis of 7.58 as such does not have a distinctly theological function. To be specific: the mention of Saul plays an important role, since it surreptitiously introduces the one who will become the main character of the story: however, the introduction of the character by means of an analepsis does not as such assume a theological function. The analeptic procedure is justified for reasons of narrative strategy, since it allows the dramatic tension to increase by presenting a Saul who is a threat to the community ('But Saul laid waste the church'). This will make all the more explosive the reversal that comes about as a result of his conversion on the Damascus road (Acts 9).

In the very frequent cases in biblical literature in which the narrative manoeuvre of anachrony has above all theological reasons, we can distinguish anachronies by the context in which they apply: individual, social, socio-religious or cultural.

1. Anachrony rooted in the individual history of a character

During the reign of David the ark was still installed in the middle of a tent. The king then formed the plan of building a temple in which it would be put (II Sam.7.1). The prophet Nathan, initially enthusiastic about this idea, returns to David and delivers the following message from God: 'I took you from the pasture, from following the sheep, that you should be prince over Israel, my people. . .' (7.8). Here the analepsis touches on a new development in the action: the prophet, after reminding the king of his humble origins and the divine initiative in his social ascent, tells him that it is not for him to build a house for the Lord. The opposite will happen: 'Moreover the Lord declares to you that the Lord will make you a house. . . I will raise up your offspring after you, who shall come forth from your body, and I will establish his kingdom. He shall build a house for my name' (7.11–13). The analepsis on the individual history of David recalls a central truth: God keeps the initiative; he does not allow himself to be shut up in a house built with human hands. He alone will establish the dynasty of David against his enemies. There is the same accent on the

MORDECAI'S DREAM

The content of the canonical book of Esther is well known: Esther, a young Jewish woman among the exiles, becomes queen of Persia. Her cousin and tutor, Mordecai, discovers a plot against the king's life. Esther intervenes in the threat which has been posed, risking her own life (the grand vizier Haman tries to suppress the Jews). Thanks to the courageous intervention of the queen, Haman ends by being hanged. The book concludes with the institution of the Feast of Lots (Purim) in memory of this deliverance.

Most translations reproduce the Hebrew text of the book of Esther. But there is a very old Greek text, with many amplifications by comparison with the Hebrew version. These Greek additions are interesting from a narratological point of view, since at two strategic points in the narrative they present a dream of Mordecai: at the beginning of the book (a prefiguration of what is going to happen) and as a closure (an interpretation of the dream in the light of the events which have taken place). Prolepsis and analepsis.

Here is the first addition in the Greek text:

In the second year of the reign of Artaxerxes the Great, on the first day of Nisan, Mordecai had a dream. . .: Behold, noise and confusion, thunders and earthquake, tumult upon the earth. And behold, two great dragons came forward, both ready to fight, and they roared terribly. And at their roaring every nation prepared for war, to fight against the nation of the righteous. And behold, a day of darkness and gloom, tribulation and distress, affliction and great tumult upon the earth! And the whole righteous nation was troubled; they feared the evils that threatened them, and were ready to perish. Then they cried to God; and from their cry, as though from a tiny spring, there came a great river, with abundant water; light came, and the sun rose, and the lowly were exalted and consumed those held in honour. Mordecai saw in this dream what God had determined to do, and after he awoke he had it on his mind and sought all day to understand it in every detail (Greek Esther A,1–11).

The dream is a premonition. Put at the beginning of the book, it is an important prolepsis for understanding the events to come: overthrow, oppression, battle, victory, fall, rise, liberation and joy. The eschatological scope is strongly marked ('Behold, a day of darkness and gloom'). Apart from this eschatological orientation, the prolepsis develops three major themes.

1. The theme of the just nation against which every people prepares to make war (v.6). This nation is shaken to its foundations, to the verge of total annihilation (v.8). In the face of this threat the threatened nation cries to God (in *Greek Esther* the names of *God* or the *Lord* appear forty-two times, while the Hebrew text never mentions God).

2. The theme of exaltation and humbling. In v.10 the dream concludes with these words: 'and the lowly were exalted and consumed those held in honour.' Exaltation follows fall for the 'just nation', but the opposite fate awaits its enemies.

3. The idea of 'consuming those held in honour' introduces the reader to another important theme in the book: 'eating'. A first festival is organized by Artaxerxes in chapter 1. Esther plans a second for the king and for Haman in chapter 7. Then in chapter 9 a festival is instituted to commemorate the liberation of the Jewish people:

Here is the interpretation of the dream, given at the end of the story:

And Mordecai said, 'These things have come from God. For I remember the dream that I had concerning these matters, and none of them has failed to be fulfilled. The tiny spring which became a river, and there was light and the sun and abundant water – the river is Esther, whom the king married and made queen. The two dragons are Haman and myself. The nations are those that gathered to destroy the name of the Jews. And my nation, this is Israel, who cried out to God and were saved. The Lord has saved his people; the Lord has delivered us from all these evils; God has done great signs and wonders, which have not occurred among the nations. For this purpose he made two lots, one for the people of God and one for all the nations. And these two lots came to the hour and moment and day of decision before God and among all the nations. And God remembered his people and vindicated his inheritance. So they will observe these days in the month of Adar, on the fourteenth and fifteenth of that month, with an assembly and joy and gladness before God, from generation to generation for ever among his people Israel (Greek Esther F 1–10).

Apart from the symbolic dimension, which is of interest (the river symbolizes Esther, whom the king has married and made queen; the two dragons represent Haman and Mordecai), two essential elements are integrated into this recapitulation.

1. Mordecai begins by confirming the divine origin of the events that have taken place. The initial dream is an evident demonstration. The Greek text of Esther thus accentuates the religious and sacred character of this history told around the Diaspora.

2. In this re-reading of events, Mordecai reconsiders the institution of the festival (already mentioned in chapter 9). In this kind of summary the narrator bases himself on the miraculous events which have just taken place (analepsis) to justify the institution of a commemoration (prolepsis). The Feast of Lots is thus given a religious origin and stamp. The writing is addressed to a faith community which is already celebrating a commemorative festival.

On the narrative level, the initial prolepsis of Greek Esther projects the reader into the world of the story by offering the decipherment of a mysterious dream. This exercise corresponds perfectly to the literary taste of the era.

On the theological level, the essential function of the final analepsis is to confirm the divine origin of the events reported in the narrative (salvation of the threatened people obtained through the influence of Queen Esther).

---

divine initiative in John 21.18 (the prolepsis on the martyr death of Peter).

not alarmed; for this must take place, but the end is not yet.'

2. Anachrony linked to the social context

Some anachronies allude to a situation of oppression and collective suffering. Thus the dramatic analepsis of Matt.23.35: 'That upon you may come all the righteous blood shed on earth, from the blood of innocent Abel to the blood of Zechariah the son of Barachiah, whom you murdered between the sanctuary and the altar.' Or Luke 13.1: 'There were some present at that very time who told him of the Galileans whose blood Pilate had mingled with their sacrifices.' In this analepsis in the Lukan account Jesus makes use of a different fact on which to base a catechesis on conversion.

The context of collective suffering shines through in the prolepsis of Matt.24.6: 'And you will hear of wars and rumours of wars. See that you are

3. Anachrony on the social and religious level

Jacob 'limped because of his thigh. Therefore to this day the Israelites do not eat the sinew of the hip which is upon the hollow of the thigh' (Gen.32.32–33). The evocation of the narrator's present is a prolepsis in relation to the story; this 'leap into the future' shows the importance of the link established between an event and a custom which has its origin in it. For the readers the past and the present are linked: the experience of the patriarch is transposed into their lives through the dietary prohibition.

We can see a parallel set of problems in a text of Exodus. At the exodus from Egypt Moses addresses the elders of Israel: 'And when you come to the land which the Lord will give you, as he has promised, you shall keep this service. And when your children say to you, "What do you mean by this service?", you shall say, "It is the sacrifice of the Lord's Passover, for he passed over the houses of the people of Israel in Egypt, when he slew the Egyptians but spared our houses"' (Ex.12.26–27). The function of the prolepsis is to remind the people that the divine promise will certainly be accomplished: 'When you enter Canaan you will observe . . .' But it is worth noting that it is combined with an analepsis: in the explanation given to the descendants it will be necessary to refer to the day when the Lord passes over the houses of the people of Israel in Egypt.' The text is thus double confirmation of the word of God, since the event to which allusion is made retrospectively (protection of the Israelites at the time of the tenth plague) has not yet happened when Moses pronounces these words. On the other hand, he inculcates a central notion into the people: the intensive cultivation of memory of the past.

4. Anachrony taking place on the cultural level

This type of anachrony is particularly interesting. It mainly includes quotations, whether explicit or not, and allusions to words or events known to all. Announcing the day when the Son of man will reveal himself, Jesus, having exhorted his followers not to turn back, ends in these terms: 'Remember Lot's wife' (Luke 17.32). We begin from quite a distant future (the great day seen in the light of the history of salvation, peculiar to Luke) and we go back a very long way in time (the time of Abraham). Here the analepsis displays two features: considerable force and weak amplitude (Lot's wife meets her fate in a moment). One situation of distress is related to another, in a distant past, doubtless because of the evocative power of the punishment of Sodom (and of Lot's wife, attached to this city). The allusion is brief, but all-encompassing.

An application: John 11

The Fourth Gospel is a master of the art of anachrony. The story called 'the raising of Lazarus'

(not a good name, since it is more a matter of reviving the faith of Martha and Mary) in chapter 11 alone allows us to take account of it. Here we meet three categories of analepsis and a series of prolepses.

The first analepses emphasize the **amazing absence of Jesus** at the moment of the death of his friend Lazarus (see v.6: 'When he heard that he was ill, he stayed two days longer in the place where he was'). This absence is retrospectively underlined five times in the sequel to the story: 'Jesus found that Lazarus had already been in the tomb four days' (v.17); 'Many of the Jews had come to Martha and Mary to console them concerning their brother' (v.19); 'Lord, if you had been here, my brother would not have died' (vv.21 and 32); 'But some of them said: "Could not he who opened the eyes of the blind man have kept this man from dying"' (v.37). Here the narrative procedure of flashback emphasizes the incomprehension at Jesus' behaviour: to human sight, he should have intervened on behalf of Lazarus when Lazarus was still alive. The repetitive effect of these analepses circumscribes the theme of the narrative for the reader: what explanation can there be of the friends of Jesus dying without the intervention of the Master?

The second type of analepsis relates to the **sending of the Son**: 'I know that you always hear me, but I have said this on account of the people standing by, that they may believe that you have sent me' (v.42). The interpreter can see an internal analepsis here: Jesus comments on his own words to make the crowd understand that he has been sent by God. But it is equally possible to discern an external analepsis here, if Jesus is alluding to the divine plan to send the Son. Thus the present situation (Jesus as sent by the Father) is based on a plan prior to any narrative; and it is this past which gives the present its decisive character.

The third type of analepsis is very much more subtle, since it is a proleptic analepsis. It concerns **the identification of Mary** through an explicit commentary by the narrator (> 8.1): 'It was Mary *who anointed the Lord with ointment and wiped his feet with* *her hair*, whose brother Lazarus was ill' (v.2). Now the anointing at Bethany is not reported by the same narrator until the next chapter (12.1–11)! Why confer a prior status ('who had anointed') on a gesture which the narrative has not yet presented? Scholars have formulated the hypothesis of a reversal of the order of the chapters, but without carrying conviction. From a narratalogical point of view we are no longer at the level of the story but at the level of narrativization, where the narrator directly addresses the readers. These know, by virtue of their culture, what role Mary played at the beginning of the story of the passion; this role was in fact anchored in the tradition before this Gospel was composed. So the narrator can appeal to the memory of his readers and tell them about Mary in the pluperfect, denoting an anteriority which does not function on the level of the story but on the level of the dialogue with the reader. Thus the analepsis functions in the reader's mind, but at the level of the story it takes on a proleptic colour.

Three internal prolepses are dispersed through the narrative. Their function is to indicate the significance that the death of Lazarus will take on, or to show Jesus' determination the moment his friend is dead. 'When Jesus heard it, he said, "This illness is not unto death; it is for the glory of God, so that the Son of God may be glorified by means of it"' (v.4). 'Our friend Lazarus is asleep, but I am going to wake him' (v.11). 'Thomas, called the Twin, said to his fellow disciples, "Let us also go, that we may die with him!"' (v.16). These three incursions into the near future emphasize the difference in perception which is evident between Jesus, informed of the divine plan, and the disciples, filled with fear and incomprehension.

A great final prolepsis (vv.47–53) reports the plans made by the chief priests and the Pharisees following the miracle. We should note three strong emphases: 1. the fear that the Romans will intervene and destroy the holy place and the nation (v.48); 2. Caiaphas' suggestion (it is expedient that one man should die for the people and that the whole nation should not perish); 3. the double meaning that the narrator wants to give these words, so that they can be read as a prophecy of the saving and universal force of the death of Jesus. The allusion to the possible intervention of the Romans largely falls outside the setting of the story, while the allusion to the death of Jesus remains within it. This prolepsis is of a *mixed* type, both external and internal. If the prolepsis in v.4 unveiled the divine plan through the mouth of Jesus, that in v.51 makes the narrator himself interpret the meaning of the death of Jesus: these incursions into the future are decisive for orientating the theological reception of the narrative through the reader.

Their importance increases yet again if we note the central prolepsis of the narrative (11.22–26): the debate between Martha and Jesus on the resurrection. It is worth measuring Jesus' argument in terms of a shift in Martha's mind. For her the resurrection takes place on the last day (v.24); the future is distant (external prolepsis). For Jesus, on the contrary, the resurrection is a reality to be lived out immediately which begins in the present (internal prolepsis).

Check your knowledge

- On their way to the promised land the Hebrew people are refused passage by the Edomites. What is the force of the analepsis of Num. 20.15–16?
- In Gen 40.12–15, Joseph interprets the dream of Pharaoh's cupbearer. Note the prolepses and analepses in these verses and specify their force.
- In Gen.22.8, Abraham declares to his son Isaac: 'God will provide the lamb for the sacrifice, my son.' What is the force of this prolepsis?
- Deuteronomy 26 relates the institution of the rite of the firstfruits. Note the analepses and prolepses in the story. What is their force and their amplitude? What significance do they give to the rite?

DEFINITIONS

Anachrony: discord between the order of the narrative (narrative discourse) and the order of the story, from the point of view of the disposition of events or temporal segments. There are two types of anachrony, analepsis and prolepsis. The anachrony can be internal (to the story), external (to the temporal segment of the story), or mixed (external and internal). It can be heterodiegetic (relating to a narrative line different from the first) or homodiegetic (completing a lacuna prior to the story or filling in, in advance, a later gap in the story).

Analepsis: a flashback evoking at a later stage an event which is anterior from the point of view of the story. The analepsis can be internal, eternal or mixed (see *anachrony*).

Prolepsis: a narrative manoeuvre which consists in anticipating or relating in advance an event which is later from the point of view of the story. The prolepsis can be internal, external or mixed (see *anachrony*).

So the whole story in John 11 can be grasped as a narrative movement, which, encountering distress before death, shifts the hope of the believer by making it pass from being distant (external to the narrative) to being very close (internal to the narrative).

Finally, a study of the anachronies draws the attention of the readers to their own capacities for recollection and anticipation. We shall touch on these capacities (memorial and previsional) later; they are basic to the work of reading (> 9.3).

7.3 Frequency

The narrator's play with time goes on. Now we approach it from the aspect of frequency. Several scenarios need to be envisaged. The narrator can relate x times something that has happened once: this is the *repetitive* narrative. He can relate once something that has happened x times; this is the *iterative* narrative. He can also adopt a strict correspondence between the occurrence of the event and the narrative occurrence, telling once (or twice or three times) something that has happened once (or twice or three times): that is the *singulative* narrative. We shall begin with that.

The singulative narrative

A narrative is *singulative* when the narrator relates once what has happened once (or x times what has happened x times). The single narrative about the single event is clearly the most frequent case in the biblical narration.

In the case of plural mentions of events, the narrative effect of the repetition must be observed carefully. Contrary to first impressions, the threefold announcement of the passion-resurrection of Jesus is not narrativized as a repetitive narrative. The effect of prolepsis is evident. But after the announcement in Mark 8.31, the narrator does not repeat this first prediction in 9.31 and 10.33–34; he relates how Jesus twice and on different occasions reiterates the proleptic announcement of his death. A detailed comparison of the three announcements will show a gradation from the first to the third, again dramatized by the approach to Jerusalem. Alerted by the first, readers will carefully note the gravity which develops with the second announcement; the third stylistically adopts a hammering effect which definitively impresses on their minds the horror to come.

In the book of Numbers the Hebrew Bible presents a far less well known scene which is also repeated three times: the oracles given by Balaam in

SINGULATIVE NARRATIVE

the presence of king Balak, who has ordered him to curse the people of Israel. First Balaam pronounces his incantation (23.7–10), at which Balak is furious; instead of cursing his enemies, Balaam has showered them with blessings. This gives the king the following idea: 'Come with me to another place from which you may see this people – you will see only part of them, you will not see them all. Then curse them for me from there' (23.13). The scene is repeated on the summit of Pisgah. Then Balaam pronounces his second incantation (vv.18–24), which leads to an immediate reprimand from Balak: 'If you do not curse them, at least do not bless them' (23.25). Balak then makes a third attempt and leads Balaam to the summit of Peor. There he offers a sacrifice and Balaam pronounces his third incantation (24.3–9). Balak finally becomes furious and says to him in anger: 'I called you to curse my enemies and behold, you have blessed them these three

times. I said I would certainly honour you, but the Lord has held you back from honour' (24.10–11). This triple incantation, pronounced three times in the story and reported three times in the narrativization, produces a gripping rhetorical effect of powerlessness: despite the obstinacy of the king of the Moabites, Balaam succeeds only in showering Israel with blessings. The constraint exercised by God is suggested by Balaam's triple declaration, which can be summed up thus: 'When I speak, must I not keep to what the Lord puts in my mouth?' We are very close to the effect of narrative redundancy that the repetitive narrative has.

The repetitive narrative

The term *repetitive* is kept for the narrative which relates x times what has happened once.

The most striking example is in the Acts of the

DEFINITIONS

Singulative narrative: a narrative relating once a single event in the story (the most common state).

Repetitive narrative: a narrative returning several times to a single event in the story.

Iterative narrative: a narrative mentioning once something that has happened several times in the story.

REPETITIVE NARRATIVE

Apostles, where the scene of the confession of Saul of Tarsus is related three times with notable differences. The first time the experience is related by the narrator in the third person (9.1–25). The second narrative is a speech by Paul to the Jews of Jerusalem (22.1–21) in which the apostle justifies his mission in Gentile territory. The third is also a plea by Paul, but in front of king Agrippa (26.1–23). This repetition lends considerable weight to the event in the economy of the book of Acts; in Luke's eyes Paul's calling in fact gives concrete expression to the continuity and change between the history of the fathers and the new faith in Jesus.

But the narrative redundancy does not make its effect solely by repetition; it also makes it by difference, since to repeat is not to keep pace with. The presentation of the events on the Damascus road changes from one version to another. The first tendency in the change is a progressive concentration on the encounter between Paul and Jesus: from Acts 9 to Acts 26 the details of Paul's experience are progressively effaced (his blinding, his baptism); the secondary characters (Anaanias, Barnabas) disappear to such a degree that chapter 26 leaves only Paul and Jesus face to face. The second change consists in varying the point of view: each time, although the narrator is reporting the same event, he changes the perspective. In Acts 9 he brings out the importance of the intermediaries who have been necessary in the conversion of Saul (his travelling companions, Ananias, Barnabas). In the speech of Acts 22 the conversion serves to demonstrate the basic continuity between Paul's Jewish past and his faith in Christ. In Acts 26, the conversion

ITERATIVE NARRATIVE

makes concrete the action of the risen Christ in Paul's life, with a view to establishing the connection between the new faith and Pharisaic belief in the resurrection.

Thus the author of Acts succeeds in integrating the experience of the apostle into the global history of the first Christian community while exploiting the different facets of the event.

The iterative narrative

The *iterative* narrative relates once something that has happened x times. Such a narrative concentration generally takes place on the edges of the plot, i.e. in the statement of the initial situation or the final situation (> 4.2). It also allows the transition between two scenes. The *summary* is a good example of the iterative narrative (>7.1).

I Samuel 1.1–3 opens both the first book of Samuel and the scene of the meeting between Hannah and the priest Eli. 'There was a man of Ramathaim Zophim in the hill-country of Ephraim. He was called Elkanah. . . He had two wives, one was called Hannah and the other Peninah. Peninah had children but Hannah did not. Every year, this man went up from his city to worship the Lord and to sacrifice to him at Shiloh. . .' Luke 4.16 is the threshold of a scene in which Jesus preaches at the synagogue in Nazareth. Jesus 'came to Nazareth where he had been brought up. On the sabbath *according to his custom* he entered the synagogue, and stood up to read.' In both cases the iterativity establishes in the narrative an initial state that the story will set out to dramatize (this is the role of the complication).

The book of Job also opens with an iterative narrative (Job 1.4–5), showing Job's piety after the first verses of the book have told us that he is just in the eyes of God (for these concepts > 5.7).

For iterative narratives making a transition between two scenes see Ex.40.36–38 or I Kings 9.25 or II Sam.5.13–15, or again Mark 4.33–34; Luke 3.40; 8.1–3; 19.47–48, etc.

Check your knowledge

- The crossing of the Red Sea is related in Ex.13.17–14.31 and then sung in the song of Miriam and Moses (Ex.15). What effect of coupling is thus produced?
- Make a careful comparison between the three narratives of the meeting between Peter and Cornelius in Acts 10.9–48; Acts 11.5–18 and Acts 15.7–11. What elements are hidden, summed up, transformed or underlined between one version and another?

For further reading

J. Bres, *La Narrativité*, Louvain-la Neuve: Duculot 1994, 43–72 and 119–43 (concord and discord between time and narrative).

G. Genette, *Figures* III, Paris: Editions du Seuil 1972, 71–224 (temporality in the narrative).

G. Genette, *Nouveau discours du récit*, Paris: Editions du Seuil 1983, 15–27 (temporality in the narrative: debate with other narratologists).

J. L. Ska, *'Our Fathers Have Told Us'*, Subsidia Biblica 13, Rome: Pontificio Istituto Biblico 1990, 7–15 (synthetic presentation of Genette's concepts).

H. Weinrich, *Le Temps. Le récit et le commentaire*, Paris: Editions du Seuil 1973 (theorization on time told and time telling).

Christian Rohlfs, *The Return of the Prodigal Son*, 1916.

8

The narrative voice and its whisperings

What is the narrative voice? It is a voice which strives to guide readers by providing them with all kinds of clarifications that they need to understand the texts. These aids to understanding are the *explicit commentaries* that the narrator makes in the course of the story. We touched on the phenomenon in mentioning the evaluative point of view which induces empathy, sympathy or antipathy towards the characters in the reader (> 5.6). But this voice can also be softer, more discreet and take the form of a whisper: the reader must then learn to perceive the *implicit commentaries* provided by the narrator. It is hardly necessary to emphasize that it is crucial to grasp correctly these more or less discreet signals which programme the reading of the narrative. More than anything else they communicate the value system of the implicit author.

8.1 The explicit commentary

In guiding the reading, the narrator can achieve his aim by comments openly inserted into the narrative. We can distinguish two procedures. Either the narrator appeals directly to the reader, which amounts to a massive intrusion; in this case he brings about a temporal shift in relation to the story. Or the narrator limits himself to completing, by means of an explanatory gloss, information which is thought to be insufficient in itself.

Let the reader understand!

The *apostrophe* is the most direct form of intrusion by the narrator. The procedure is rare in biblical narration. It appears in Mark 13.14 (taken up by Matt.24.15): 'When you see the desolating sacrilege set up where it ought not to be (let the reader understand!) then let those who are in Judaea flee to the mountains.' The intrusion is clearly stronger than in the numerous cases of an imperative injunction (for example at the beginning or end of the parables): 'Listen' (Mark 4.3), 'Whoever has ears to hear let him hear' (Mark 4.9). 'Hear me and understand' (Mark 7.14). Readers can certainly feel addressed; but they can also limit the appeal to the level of the story and consider the warning an injunction on the part of the second narrator (Jesus), addressed to his listeners (the characters of the story). The situation is not the same in 13.14: the appeal to the *reader* prohibits restricting the injunction to Jesus' audience.

By all the evidence here, the narrator is intervening directly on the axis of communication. Besides, this is the only passage in the Gospel in which the narrator treats the narratee so brutally. Ordinarily it is difficult to draw a distinction between the parentheses of the narrator and the parentheses of the main character; here the difference is sharp. The marked intervention by the narrator is a strong signal to the receivers to invite them to decipher the identity of the desolating sacrilege. Relatively speaking, this direct intrusion which telescopes a

THE NARRATIVE VOICE:
A WAY OF ENLIGHTENING THE READER

way round via the characters is precisely like a phone call from a superior disregarding intermediaries.

Summing up the situation

The same concern to activate communication comes through clearly in Deut.34.5–6, where the narrator, without directly addressing the reader, *sums up the situation* in his time. He uses a temporal shift which does not pass unnoticed: 'Moses, the servant of the Lord, died there in the country of Moab, as the Lord had said. He was buried in the valley, in the country of Moab, opposite Beth-peor, and no one knows his tomb to this day.' The historical setting from which the narrative speaks ('this day') dates from several centuries after the death of Moses.

There is the same jump in time in Matt.28.15, with the same expression 'to this day', when we are told

of the guards on Jesus' tomb being bribed by the high priests: 'They took the money and did as they were directed, and this story has been spread among the Jews to this day.' The author firmly jumps from the time of the story to his own time. Addressing his first readers, he builds a bridge between former times and the time of the reading. The aim is polemical: the narrator Matthew seeks to counter the rumours circulating in his time that the corpse of Jesus had been stolen.

Crossing the thickness of time

It can even happen that the narrator provides the interpretation of a saying and depicts the *historical character of its reception*. John 2.19–22 is a good example of this: 'Jesus said to them, "Destroy this temple, and in three days I will raise it up." The Jews then said, "It has taken forty-six years to build this temple, and will you raise it up in three days?" (*wrong interpretation*). But he spoke of the temple of his body (*right interpretation*). When therefore he was raised from the dead his disciples remembered that he had said this; and they believed the scripture and the word that Jesus had spoken (*reception history*).'

By this explicit commentary the readers cross the thickness of time, as they have to for the misunderstanding to give place to a real grasp of the sayings of Jesus as illuminated by the resurrection. This Johannine reminiscence of the sayings of Jesus and their correct relocation works in connection with scripture and under the guidance of the Spirit (cf. 14.26). The same can be said of John 12.16: 'His disciples did not understand this at the time, but when Jesus was glorified, then they remembered that this had been written of him and had been done to him.'

Whether we have an apostrophe to the reader, a summary of the situation in the author's time or the historical reception of a saying, each time there is an important temporal shift, a jump from the time of the story to a later period (usually that of the narrator). When the explicit commentary is not accompanied by this shift, we have a different type of commentary: the explanatory gloss.

The explanatory gloss

A gloss is an added commentary. There are various possible glosses: scriptural arguments, explanation, translation, inside view and view from the back, evaluation.

1. **Scriptural arguments**. In particular these punctuate the beginning of the Gospel according to Matthew. After reporting the announcement made to Joseph, the narrator goes on: 'All this took place to fulfil what the Lord had spoken by the prophet: *"Behold a virgin shall conceive and bear a son, and his name shall be called Emmanuel"'* (1.22–23). After the narrative of the flight into Egypt, Matthew says: 'And he remained there until the death of Herod. This was to fulfil what the Lord had spoken by the prophet, *"Out of Egypt have I called my son!"'* (2.15). Two verses later, after the mention of the massacre of the children in Bethlehem: 'Then was fulfilled what was spoken by the prophet Jeremiah*: "A voice was heard in Ramah, wailing and loud lamentation, Rachel weeping for her children; she refused to be consoled, because they were no more"'* (2.17–18). Finally, after the death of Herod, Joseph 'went and dwelt in a city called Nazareth, that what was spoken by the prophets might be fulfilled, *"He shall be called a Nazarene"'* (2.23).

This flurry of quotations from the scriptures hammers home the same message: nothing is due to chance: the events (even the tragic ones) which surround the birth of the child-God have been predicted and have a place in the divine plan. The procedure of recourse to the scriptures has already been evaluated from the perspective of temporality; the invocation of the past is in fact a clear analepsis (> 7.2). But these analepses are inserted into the narrative by means of an explanatory gloss: 'all that happened so that. . .', 'then was fulfilled what was said. . .' Matthew, who in this way appeals to his readers' memory of scripture, glosses the narrative of events to instil his interpretation of the appearance of Jesus: to be understood properly, in his view, this appearance must be put in the line of the prophecies. In other words, Matthew grafts the plot of the 'life of Jesus' on to a unifying plot which overhangs it and gives meaning to it: the plot of the history of God with Israel (> 4.5).

2. **The explanation**. Sometimes, a narrative reports an event which the reader does not know where to place without an explanation. That is the case in II Kings 20.12: 'At that time Merodach-baladan, son of Baladan, king of Babylon, sent letters and presents to Hezekiah. . .' Why such a delegation? Why the letters and presents? The reader would never guess did not the author add, '. . .for he had learned that Hezekiah had been sick'. So it is the illness of the king of Judah which motivates the sending of the delegation. The parallel text in Isa.39.1 even provides an element of supplementary explanation: '. . .for he had learned that Hezekiah had been sick and that he had recovered'. This second narrator is concerned to give a lesson in geopolitical strategy: the king of Babylon, who has just regained his independence, is looking for allies against the Assyrians; he takes advantage of Hezekiah's recovery to win the king of Judah to his cause. The latter will fall into the trap of flattery, showing the ambassadors all his treasures; the prophet will bluntly show him his error (39.5–7).

The Second Gospel also teems with explanations: 'for he taught them as a man with authority and not as the scribes' (Mark 1.22); 'for they said, "He has lost his head"' (3.21); 'for Jesus said to him, "depart from this man, unclean spirit!"' (5.8); 'for she was twelve years of age' (5.42); 'for his name had become famous' (6.14); 'for Herod feared John' (and so on).

It is not always easy to detect an explanation, since it can take the form of a simple break in construction. Take Mark 7.19: in the middle of a discourse of Jesus the narrator comments to the narratee on the consequences of the teaching which is being given ('Thus he declared all food clean' – literally: *'he said to them. . . purifying all food'*). The intervention of the narrator here assumes the status of a metadiscourse, i.e. a reflection on the discourse which is in process of unfolding.

3. **Translation.** The expression which calls for explanation can be a proper name, a place name or a personal name: 'Emmanuel, which being translated is "God with us"' (Matt.1.23); 'When they arrived at the place called Golgotha, which means "place of the skull"' (Matt.27.33); 'Boanerges, which is "son of thunder"' (Mark 3.17); 'Go and wash yourself in the pool of Siloam, which means "sent"' (John 9.7); 'Acheladama, which means "field of blood"' (Acts 1.19); 'Joseph, surnamed Barnabas by the apostles, which means "man of consolation"' (Acts 4.36); 'She was called Tabitha, which being translated is "Gazelle"' (Acts 9.36); 'Elymas the magician – for that is how his name is translated' (Acts 13.8). There can equally be whole expressions in Hebrew or in Aramaic: '"*Eli, eli, lama sabachtani*", which is "My God, my God, why have you forsaken me?"' (Matt.27.46). '"*Talitha cumi*", which means "Little girl, I say to you, arise"' (Mark 5.41).

On occasion the translation explains the meaning of certain words in connection with a custom which is unknown to the readers: 'they saw that some of his disciples ate with unclean hands, that is, without having washed them' (Mark 7.2). 'As it was a day of preparation, that is, an eve of the sabbath' (Mark 15.42). All these translations of terms thought obscure or of customs difficult to understand are a reflection of the cultural distance which separates the narrator or his characters from the reader whom he is addressing.

4. **The inside view and the view from the back.** In the episode in which Hezekiah receives the Babylonian delegation and lays out his treasures, the prophet Isaiah censures his vanity and tells him that his riches will be carried away to Babylon and his sons made eunuchs in the palace of the king of Babylon. The narrative ends on this note: 'Hezekiah said to Isaiah, "The word of the Lord which you have spoken is good." He told himself, "There will be peace and security in my days"' (Isa 39.8). The amazing reaction of King Hezekiah, who thinks a word of misfortune 'good', is explained by the inside view which is given last: the king remains

centred on his life and his reign. It has to be noted that this explanation concludes not only this narrative but also what is usually called *First Isaiah* (Isa.1–39). This final note can be interpreted either in a positive sense (the pious king submits to the divine will) or in a negative sense ('after me the deluge'). The narrator leaves his reader with an impression of ambivalence.

The same effect can be obtained in a setting with zero focalization (> 5.9), in the sense that an observation made by the narrator can take the place of an explanatory gloss. 'As he passed by, Jesus saw a man who was blind from birth' (John 9.1). The precision provided by two last words, which is important for the rest of the narrative, is only conceivable against a well determined background: the 'view from the back', coming from the omniscient narrator, which goes beyond time and space and which is characteristic of the narrative with zero focalization.

5. **The evaluation.** The narrative of II Chron.32, which is later than the narratives of II Kings 20 and Isa.39, stands out for its peremptory judgments addressed to Hezekiah: 'The Lord answered him and gave him a sign. But Hezekiah did not make return according to the benefit done to him, for his heart was proud. Therefore wrath came upon him and Judah and Jerusalem' (32.24–25). The evaluative commentary can go as far as to abandon any causal explanation in the strict sense. 'And so in the matter of the envoys of the princes of Babylon, who had been sent to him to inquire about the sign that had been done in the land, God left him to himself, in order to try him and to know all that was in his heart' (v.31). The Chronicler, without taking up the details of the king's experience, evokes the 'pride of his heart' and the 'trial' of which he is the object at the time of the Babylonian delegation: his rereading at a distance is combined with a theological reinterpretation.

But the evaluation often takes a positive form: 'The Lord blessed the new years of Job even more than the first. He had fourteen thousand sheep and six thousand camels. . .' (Job 42.12). The information is not just factual: the return of considerable possessions along with the birth of new children induces the idea of a return of the divine blessing.

Check your knowledge

- How does the quotation from Isaiah in Mark 1.2–3 orientate the narrative of the Gospel of Mark?
- What point of view does the Chronicler give of the story of Saul in I Chron.10.13–14?
- In the episode of the woman at the house of Simon the Pharisee (Luke 7.36–50), the narrative offers two inside views (v.39 and 49). What sense do they give to the narrative?
- What sense does the narrator give to the narrative of the wedding at Cana by the commentary in John 2.11?

Intertextuality

A detailed study has been made of this phenomenon by Julia Kristeva (*Semeiotike*). Intertextuality can be defined as a relationship of co-presence between two or more texts or, if you like, as the effective presence of a text in another text. Before being rediscovered by the linguistic sciences, it was a cardinal principle of rabbinic exegesis. The church fathers also practised this reading of scripture by scripture. 'The Bible is its own commentary,' said St Jerome. Here the whole question is to know how and by what means the authors of the texts encouraged inter-textual comparisons.

The most visible manifestation of intertextuality brings together three categories: the quotation, plagiarism and the simple allusion.

The book of Revelation teems with allusions to the Old Testament. In the inaugural vision of the Son of man in 1.10–20 we can detect no less than seven allusions to the book of Daniel:

v.13a:	one like a son of man	Dan.7.13
v.13b:	clothed with a golden girdle around his breast	Dan.10.5
v.14:	his head and his hair were as white as white wool, as white as snow	Dan.7.9
v.15:	his feet were like burnished bronze	Dan.10.6
v.17:	when I saw him, I fell at his feet as though dead	Dan.8.18; 10.15
v.18:	I am alive for evermore	Dan.4.31a; 6.27b
v.19:	what is and what is to take place hereafter	Dan 2.28, 29, 45

8.2 The implicit commentary

By the explicit commentary, the narrator speaks directly; the reader hears his voice. But communication can be established indirectly: then the narrator speaks 'tacitly' through the words and actions of the characters, through the plot. He insinuates a hidden sense, counting on the competence of the reader to perceive it. The *implicit* commentary can take numerous forms: intertextual or transcultural allusions, symbolism, polysemy sometimes leading to misunderstanding, to irony, to humour.

In the first chapter of the book of Revelation it thus becomes evident that the author is placing himself in a direct line with a tradition represented by Daniel. However, he is original in his Christian re-reading of the traditional themes of Jewish apocalyptic. In the scene involving the Son of man he is not content with borrowing slavishly features from the description that Daniel gives of this enigmatic figure (Dan.7.9,10,13,14); he draws on six different chapters of that book. If we do not pay sufficient attention to the phenomenon of intertextuality, we risk missing precious indications at the moment of interpretation.

DEFINITIONS

Explicit commentary: an intervention by the narrator, whether in a commentary on the story (interpretation, explanation, judgment) or in a direct communication to the narratee (addressing the reader).

Explanatory gloss: a commentary by the narrator explaining or qualifying an aspect or an action of the story.

Intrusion of the narrator: an intervention by the narrator in the narrative, either direct (in an extreme case, the insertion of his 'I') or indirect (by the direction of the narrative).

However, rhetoric teaches us that quotation is never a neutral enterprise. Under colour of giving expression to other discourses, the discourse quoting extends its own categories, basing itself on them. But the fragment quoted can be given several statuses: (a) the *proof quotation* refutes, defends or supports an argument by reason of its content or its author (argument from authority); (b) the *relic quotation* authenticates the discourse by a fragment of 'true discourse' which the original seal confers on it; (c) the *culture quotation* creates a complicity with the reader by keeping to shared values. The relationship which the discourse quoting weaves with the discourse quoted is thus worth looking at each time, if we want to determine what function in the argument the narrator means it to play.

For example, we see that in the explicit commentary, the presence of a quotation serves as an explanation. On the other hand, the reference to the scriptures in the implicit commentary does not heighten the potential of the text to inform; it increases its potential for argument more by resonance with a past truth which it surreptitiously introduces.

Transtextuality

It is possible to understand intertextuality in a broader sense and meet up with what Gérard Genette calls transtextuality (*Palimpsestes: la littérature au second degré*). Genette defines transtextuality as everything which 'brings a text into a relationship, manifest or secret, with other texts' (*Palimpsestes*, 7). We should also note Michael Riffaterre's definition: 'The intertext is the perception by the reader of relations between one work and others which have preceded or followed it ('La trace de l'intertexte'). This broader sense includes both the simple reminiscence and the adoption of a structure, a literary matrix, just as the *Aeneid* takes up the

---

AN EXAMPLE OF A LITTLE SUBTLETY

Everyone knows the cry of Jesus on the cross as reported by Matthew: 'Towards the third hour Jesus cried with a loud voice, "*Eli, Eli, lama sabachthani*", which is to say, "My God, my God, why have you forsaken me?"' (27.46). It is usually noted that this saying takes up Ps.22.2a.

Now it is less often said that this is not a textual quotation. Instead of writing '*Eli, Eli, lema azavthani*', the Gospels (Matt.27.46 and Mark 15.34)

modify the verb 'forsake' and use the formula '*sabachthani*', which tones it down slightly and could be translated 'Why have you left me alone?' This modification goes in the direction of expressing real distress but not despair. Here is the subtlety of indirect communication... though it presupposes an implicit reader who can compare it with the usual Aramaic version.

Odyssey, and the healing of a widow's son at Nain (Luke 7.11–17) takes up the healing of a widow's son at Zarephath (I Kings 17.17–24). The characters are not the same, the adventures are different, but the plot is similar.

Genette has subtly differentiated five types of transtextual relations between a receiver text and a source text (*Palimpsestes*, 8–12). 1. Intertextuality strictly speaking denotes the physical presence of one text in another by quotation, allusion or plagiarism; 2. Paratextuality denotes the accompaniment of a text with a title, a subtitle, a preface or an epilogue; 3. Metatextuality establishes a critical relationship with another text by commenting on it; 4. Hypertextuality is the taking up or imitating of a first text without saying so; 5. Architextuality represents the most abstract form of reference to a primordial text, which is almost imperceptible. In this enumeration the explicitation of the transtextual relationship on the part of the narrator follows a decreasing order. Genette's taxonomy should lead to a fine appreciation of the interplay of echoes and references which supports relations between the New Testament and the Old Testament beyond the manifest phenomenon of quotation.

The mirror text

The gesture of anointing at Bethany on the eve of the passion is commented on by Jesus like this: 'What she could do, she has done: she has anointed my body in advance for burial. And in truth I tell you, wherever the gospel is proclaimed throughout the world, what she has done will also be told in memory of me' (Mark 14.8–9). This comment-ary unveils the symbolic gesture of the woman who has just anointed his head: it makes this a place where the force of the passion towards which Jesus is going is concentrated. That is why this gesture will accompany the proclamation of the gospel throughout the world. It follows from this that readers, becoming aware of Mark's narrative, can immediately verify that Jesus' saying is well-founded: it is realized the moment they read it!

This procedure of turning the event back on itself has been given a name which comes from heraldry, the *mise en abyme* (or *mirror text*); originally this name denoted the miniaturized inclusion of a blazon within an encompassing coat of arms. In literary terms it denotes a discourse of the work about itself, a word about the discourse, narrative about the narrative. André Gide made it fashionable (the first allusion comes in the *Correspondence* in 1891); since then it has become popular in the New Novel. L.Dällenbach gives this definition: 'The *mise en abyme* (mirror text) is any enclave with a relationship of likeness to the work which contains it' (*Le récit spéculaire: essai sur la mise en abyme*, 18).

We are going to examine two cases of rather more complex mirror texts than the saying of Jesus about the anointing at Bethany: Jeremiah's scroll and the meeting between Peter and Cornelius in Acts 10–11.

In Jeremiah 36 the Lord gives orders to Jeremiah to get a scroll and write on it all the words that he has spoken on the subject of Israel, Judah and the nations. The public reading of this scroll, made by his secretary Baruch, upsets the people of the court who hear it. 'Then the king sent Jehudi to get the scroll, and he took it from the chamber of Elishama the secretary; and Jehudi read it to the king and all the princes who stood beside the king. It was the ninth month, and the king was sitting in the winter house and there was a fire burning in the brazier before him. As Jehudi read three or four columns, the king would cut them off with a penknife and throw them into the fire in the brazier, until the entire scroll was consumed in the fire that was in the brazier. Yet neither the king, nor any of his servants who heard all these words, was afraid, nor did they rend their garments. . . Now after the king had burned the scroll with the words which Baruch wrote at Jeremiah's dictation, the word of the Lord came to Jeremiah: "Take another scroll and write on it all the former words that were in the first school, which Jehoiakim the king of Judah has burned"' (vv.21–28).

From the fact that Jeremiah then gets hold of another scroll and that Baruch writes on it all the

THE MISE EN ABYME

words of the book burned by the king of Judah, adding to it 'many other similar words', we are led to see the first scroll, burned by Jehoiakim, as a miniaturized replica of all the prophet's work. In other words, the destruction of this document offers a gripping summary of what awaits all the prophetic writings, by their very nature, and by extension all the prophets: like Jeremiah they are thwarted, persecuted and rejected. In the end, in the 'summary' of Jeremiah 36, we are allowed to see a recapitulation of the whole history of Israel, at least the secular opposition between those sent by God and the political power (the powerful oppose the prophets). The significance of the episode of the burnt book goes far beyond that of an autobiographical story.

Jeremiah presented the case of a text within another text. In Acts 10–11, the reader comes upon a series of discourses which are repeated as in a play of mirrors (the *mise en abyme* can also be called a mirror story). This magnificent narrative has

already been touched on from the perspective of geographical setting (> 6.3). We shall return to it to appreciate its mirror structure. Cornelius' vision (10.3b-6) is recounted successively by those he sends to Peter (10.22), then by Cornelius himself (10.30–33), and finally by Peter at Jerusalem (11.12b-14). Similarly Peter's vision, related first of all by the narrator (10.10–16), is taken up in the following chapter by the one who has benefited from it (11.5–10). The multiplication of speeches reported itself evokes the proliferation of meetings and constantly repeated pieces of almost unbelievable news. At each repetition, if we look carefully, the event proves slightly different, depending on those being addressed.

But there is more. Here is the summary of the ministry of Jesus as Peter presents it to the centurion Cornelius: 'The word which was proclaimed thoughout all Judaea, beginning from Galilee after the baptism which John preached; how God anointed Jesus of Nazareth with the Holy Spirit and with power; how he went about doing good and healing all that were oppressed by the devil, for God was with him' (10.37–38). This summary of the life of Jesus is itself condensed by Peter in the next chapter in the explanation which he gives to the Christians of Jerusalem: 'And I remembered the word of the Lord, how he said, "John baptized with water, but you shall be baptized with the Holy Spirit"' (11.16).

This phrase had not been quoted at Cornelius' home, where Peter alluded only to the baptism proclaimed by John. Only after the event does Peter understand the meaning of this declaration, according to the narrator, and he keeps it in his summary. It has to be remembered that the Gospel of Luke, which contains the teaching of Jesus, forms the first part of Luke's work (Luke-Acts); the conditions of a mirror text are thus present: Peter's reminiscence shows how the gospel can be received and understood in the Christian community when it is a matter of welcoming believers of non-Jewish origin.

The paradox

Let's keep to Acts 10–11 to appreciate how a paradox can guide the structure of the narrative in the background.

The interlocking of the narratives emphasizes a state of want in the case of Cornelius. At the beginning Cornelius is described as a rich man, showering largesse on the Jewish people (10.2); however, his riches are small compared with the value that Peter holds (he is the one whom Cornelius has to invite to give him the Word). Peter also suffers from some wants: he is hungry, he does not understand the vision, he has to leave without knowing why (10.9–22); these wants will be less marked in the second narrative (11.5–12). The series of narratives interlocked and detached thus apparently creates a lack of symmetry. But the narrative strategy will work to re-establish a symmetry: how is it possible for a 'poor' man (Peter) to give to a 'rich' man (Cornelius)? The narrative brings this about by making the poor man rich (in words) and the rich

man poor (it is Cornelius who makes a request of Peter). However, the narrator has not reached the end of the paradox. The strongest part has yet to come. Cornelius will be enriched, not by what Peter gives him, but by the word of Jesus: 'You will receive baptism in the Holy Spirit' (11.16). What definitively gives meaning to the event is not Peter's speech; it is the word of Jesus, the second word, which Peter bears: that is why the apostle's discourse will be interrupted by the irruption of the Spirit which literally cuts off Peter's words (10.44). Hence the fine phrase of Louis Marin: 'It is by losing the word of truth that Peter rediscovers the truth of the word' ('Essai d'analyse structurale d'Actes 10,1–11,18', 49).

The narrative of the binding of Isaac in Genesis 22 also takes place on the basis of paradox. God requires Abraham to sacrifice Isaac, the son of the promise. Now after the calling of Abraham (Gen.12) and the announcement of a posterity (Gen.18), after all the vicissitudes which have separated the promise from its realization, the story seems to arrive at its happy ending in chapter 21. But at this point everything is put in question, and the readers think that they are watching the disintegration of what has gone before: the collapse no longer seems to have been caused by human weaknesses but by God, who withdraws what he has given. The whole context of the narrative cycle of Abraham pushes the paradox to an extreme. The first paradox is that the God who has promised the posterity demands the sacrifice of the son. The second paradox is that

Check your knowledge

- In what and how can the episode of Jesus at Nazareth (Luke 4.16–30) be considered a mirror text in the work of Luke as a whole?
- In putting the question to the lawyer who has questioned him (Luke 10.36), Jesus makes the Samaritan the neighbour of the wounded man and not vice versa; how is this paradox to be understood?

while showing himself ready to sacrifice Isaac, Abraham has to love him and also love the God who gives this order. Without this double paradox the dramatic recourse of the narrative is relaxed.

The misunderstanding

'Language is a source of misunderstandings', recalls the fox in *The Little Prince*. Experience confirms how well founded this statement is. The biblical narration also plays on this truth.

The narrative can exploit misunderstandings for theological ends. When Jesus has just cried out *'Eli, Eli, lema sabachthani'*, the First Gospel notes what is said next: 'Some of those who were there said on hearing it, "He is calling on Elijah!" Immediately one of them ran with a sponge which he soaked in vinegar, and fixing it to the end of a reed, he offered it to him to drink. Others said, "Listen! Let us see if Elijah will come to save him." But Jesus, crying out again in a loud voice, yielded up the spirit' (Matt.27.47–50). The linguistic misunderstanding deepens the solitude of the character.

The plot of the narrative can be constructed on a misunderstanding. The story of Balaam is even built on a double misunderstanding, since on the one hand Balaam 'forces God's hand' (Num.22.10–12, 19–20), so that God has to remind him of his mission (the episode of the ass: 22.21–35); on the other hand Balak expects Balaam to do precisely what he expects of him, but Balaam will have to confess his impotence to curse the people of God (Num. 24.12–13).

The misunderstanding can also be used as a rhetorical procedure to alert the readers and indicate to them wrong ways of understanding: that is the case in the Fourth Gospel.

Symbolism

The reader of the Fourth Gospel cannot fail to notice the importance of symbolic language in it. It is flooded with metaphors applied to Christ: he is the living water, the light of the world, the bread of heaven, the lamb of God, the good shepherd, the vine, the way, the truth, the life – all these christological metaphors have found their way into Christian language. In John the symbolic language shares in a triple function along with misunderstandings and irony: *first*, it functions through the connivance of the reader (who knows that the metaphor is to be taken in the figurative sense); *secondly*, the symbol has a didactic aim (it teaches through the image which is Christ); *thirdly*, it teaches the reader how to read the Gospel (it is after hearing Jesus say in 8.12 'I am the light of the world' that the reader will understand what is at issue in the healing of the man born blind in chapter 9).

Let's look more closely at the way in which a narrative constructs its internal symbolism: the story of the tower of Babel in Genesis 11.1–9. Basic oppositions support the narrative and make the plot develop: 1. Regrouping, dispersion; 2. Union/ dissension.

The *regrouping* is evoked by the following mentions: 'the whole earth' (v.1), 'a plain in the land of Shinar' (v.2), 'a city and a tower' (v.4), 'a name' (v.4). The theme of the *dispersion* is expressed as such in v.4 (fear expressed by humans) and then in vv.8 and 9 (divine punishment for their totalitarian plan). The *union* is transparent in the cascade of imperatives in vv.3 and 4: 'let us go', 'let us make bricks', 'let us burn', 'let us build', and above all the significant expression 'let us make a name for ourselves'; it is taken up and echoed in the reflection attributed to God in v.6: 'They are all one people and they have all one language.' The dissension results directly from the action of the Lord: 'Come, let us go down and there confuse their language, that they may no longer understand one another's speech' (v.7). It forms the object of the etymology proposed in v.9 to explain the name of Babel (here attached to the root *balal*: confound, trouble, confuse).

How does the narrative in Gen.11 construct its symbolism?

First of all on the geographical level. The 'whole earth' evoked at the beginning gives way to a precise place, 'a plain in the land of Shinar', but the

THE FOURTH GOSPEL AND ITS MISUNDERSTANDINGS

The narrative technique of misunderstanding is systematically exploited in the Fourth Gospel. The scheme is always the same: Jesus makes a declaration which is ambiguous, either because it is figurative or because it contains a hidden meaning. Those who hear it interpret it literally, or rebel against his declaration. Most frequently the correct explanation is then provided by Jesus or (less frequently) by the narrator.

In chapter 4, Jesus engages in a dialogue with a Samaritan woman beside Jacob's well: '"*Every one who drinks of this water will thirst again, but whoever drinks of the water that I shall give him will never thirst; the water that I shall give him will become in him a spring of water welling up to eternal life." The woman said to him, "Sir, give me this water, that I may not thirst, nor come here to draw*"' (John 4.13–15). Polarized on the recipient, on the depth of the well and the comings and goings necessary to get water, the Samaritan woman does not grasp the mysterious hidden sense of Jesus' words. Only much later on, in another micro-narrative, will the enigma be unveiled: '*If any one thirst, let him come to me and drink. He who believes in me, as the scripture has said, "Out of his heart shall flow rivers of living water*"' (7.37b-38).

Thus Jesus' mission is also open to misunderstanding. When Jesus says 'he who has sent me', the reader familiar with the Gospel immediately understands this theological designation. But Jesus' interlocutors, at the level of the story, are constantly mistaken. '*Jesus then said, "I shall be with you a little longer, and then I go to him who sent me; you will seek me and you will not find me; where I am you cannot come." The Jews said to one another, "Where does this man go that we shall not find him? Does he intend to go to the Dispersion among the Greeks and teach the Greeks? What does he mean by saying "You will seek me and you will not find me," and "Where I am you cannot come"?*"' (7.33–36). '*Again Jesus said to them, "I go away, and you will seek me and die in your sin; where I am going you cannot come." Then said the Jews, "Will*

he kill himself, since he says, "Where I am going you cannot come?"' (8.21–22).

These two last quotations allow us to grasp precisely the mechanism of the misunderstanding. 1. The incomprehension arises from expressions which are to be taken figuratively ('where I am', 'where I am going') which Jesus' interlocutors understand in the strict sense. 2. Readers familiar with the Fourth Gospel comprehend that there is a misunderstanding; so the misunderstanding is part of a language for initiates, and this gives the reader a position superior to that of the characters in the story (> 3.8). 3. The point is that without knowing it, the interlocutors of Jesus are speaking the truth: Jesus will in fact address the Greeks (the Jews of the Diaspora), but not as his audience understand this; Jesus will in fact give his life, but this will not be suicide.

If we examine all the Johannine misunderstandings, we will see that the procedure is attached to certain central points of the Johannine christology: the death, resurrection and glorification of Jesus (2.19–21; 6.51–53; 7.33–36; 8.21–22; 12.32–34; 13.36–38; 14.4–6; 16.16–19). The other misunderstandings concern, in turn, the identity and the nature of the children of God, whether this is their 'birth' (3.3–5), the 'bread which they eat' (6.32–35), 'the water which springs up for them' (4.10–15), their 'freedom' (8.31–35), etc.

Is the function of the Johannine misunderstandings to show the reader the foolishness of those who address Jesus? Does it seek to ridicule Nicodemus, the Samaritan woman, the Jews, the disciples (since they too fall victim to misunderstanding)? To attribute a primary anti-Judaism to John is a mistake. His aim is much more profound: to understand the destiny of the Son requires a leap, a shift, a change in the image of God. The misunderstanding indicates the need for this leap without which people remain 'outside', as if deaf, understanding nothing.

'Their most obvious function is to enforce a marked distinction between "insiders" and "outsiders", between those who understand Jesus and those who do not. Explanations of the misunderstandings draw the reader further into the circle of "insiders"... A further effect of the misunderstandings is to remove any doubt or misconception about key points in John's theology... The must significant point of the misunderstandings, however, is to teach readers how to read the gospel. The misunderstandings call attention to the gospel's metaphors, double-entendres, and plurisignations' (R.A.Culpepper, *Anatomy of the Fourth Gospel* 164–5)

For further reading
D. Marguerat, *Le Dieu des premiers chrétiens*, Geneva: Labor et Fides [3]1997, 213–30).

movement of concentration does not stop there: the human beings regroup in a city, and the centre of their project consists in a tower, 'with its top in the heavens'. Thus the concentric circles on the horizontal plane result in a vertical axis which, pointing towards heaven, threatens the divine dwelling. The tower becomes the vehicle of a totalitarian plan – a challenge to the Creator.

The second symbolic element is *language*. It alone is at the service of the thoughts of greatness which are born in the human heart; it guarantees the cohesion of the plan: 'Behold, said the Lord, they are one people, and they have one language and this is only the beginning of what they will do, and nothing that they propose to do will be impossible for them' (v.6). Once it has been confused, the language will bear witness to the fact that agreement and fusional union are from now on out of reach; the difference in cultural riches has been preserved.

Thus Babel, the Gate of the gods (*Bab-ilani*) becomes the place *par excellence* of failure and confusion: that is the third element in the symbolism of the story. Polemical and satirical, it points to *Babylon*'s pretensions to universal domination. The memory of the Jewish deportation to this city makes the name Babylon very evocative; we find its symbolic force in the Jewish tradition (the book of Daniel) and in the Christian milieu (the Revelation of John) to evoke the excess of a power of disruption and oppression.

Irony

Irony is not to be confused with humour. Irony is a mode of discourse which utters falsehood to make it possible to understand the truth, without seeking a comic effect. 'Good performance,' the teacher may say to a pupil after a spectacular failure. The content of ironic discourse must thus be falsified. Readers must grasp that the opposite is true, which obliges them to reconstruct the communication which the author suggests to them.

Wayne Booth has studied the rhetorical mechanism of irony, distinguishing four stages along which the reader is led: 1. rejection of the literal sense; 2. a search for other interpretations of the given expression; 3. an evaluation of these interpretations in terms of the perception imputed to the author; 4. a semantic decision taken on the basis of the intention imputed to the author (*A Rhetoric of Irony*, 10–13).

In the biblical narratives, irony is manifested in two forms: *verbal* irony is used at the moment when someone consciously says something but thinks the opposite; *dramatic* or situational irony translates a discord between the story and the contradictory signs sent by the narrator as to its meaning.

The sharpest form of **verbal irony** is *sarcasm*. One might think of Elijah, on the summit of Mount Carmel, addressing the priests of Baal: 'Cry louder, he is a god; he is busy, he may be absent, or on a journey; perhaps he is sleeping and must be awoken' (I Kings 18.27). Let us remember in passing that the irony is not gratuitous: in Canaanite religion Baal was specifically conceived of as periodically absent, or momentarily dead, each spring marking his rebirth. The man born blind is also sarcastic at the moment when the Pharisees ask him how Jesus has opened his eyes: 'I have already told you, but you have not listened. Why do you want to hear once again? Do you too want to become his disciples?' (John 9.27).

In addition to sarcasm, verbal irony can take the form of *the irony of the test*. When Lot gets up to go to meet the two angels arriving in Sodom, he invites them, saying: 'My lords, turn aside, I pray you, to your servant's house and spend the night, and wash your feet; then you may rise up early and go on your way.' But the angels reply to him, 'No; we will spend the night in the street' (Gen.19.2). The angels are testing how serious the offer is which Lot has made them of a welcome under his roof, indicating to him the opposite of their real intention.

Verbal irony can also manifest itself by much more subtle *points*. In Mark 7 Jesus discusses the traditions with the Pharisees. After saying in v.6, '*Well* did Isaiah prophesy of you,' Jesus adds: 'You have a *fine* way of rejecting the commandments of God, in order to keep your tradition' (v.9). The same adverb, in Greek, is translated 'well' in v.6 and 'fine' in v.9. In the first case it has a non-ironic sense, but in the second it is ironical ('That's fine, what you're doing').

Dramatic (or situational) **irony** arises the moment the reader notes a discord between the story and the signals transmitted by the author in his narration. What is the function of the irony here? It is aimed at drawing the readers towards the evaluative point of view of the narrator, at leading them to share his judgment, his hierarchy of values, his view of the world, in short his ideology. As we said earlier in connection with the Johannine misunderstandings, the use of irony has an effect on the cohesion of the group-reader: 1. it helps the group to define itself, creating a distance between those who can perceive it and decipher it and those who

IRONY OF THE SITUATION

cannot; 2. because it is expressed in a veiled way, it protects its institutions and practices against external threats; 3. by its elusive character, or at least by the impossibility of grasping it immediately, it makes the language of the group easier to adapt.

The text of John 9, in which we have already indicated a verbal irony (9.27), is not short of dramatic irony. The reading of v.24 ('Give the praise to God; we know that this man is a sinner') or v.40 ('Are we also blind?') clearly shows this. In the first case, inviting the blind man to speak the truth in the face of God, the Pharisees would have to be supporting the opposite of their knowledge: to heal a blind man is not a sign of sin. In the second case they are tragically confessing the truth: to reject the one who has healed the blind man bears witness to their own blindness. The narrator brings out the irony by orchestrating a discord between their discourse and the situation of healing.

The evangelist Mark is also a craftsman in situational irony. Among the innumerable possibilities, we shall limit ourselves to looking at a scene in the passion: Peter's denial (Mark 14.66–72). It is at the moment when Jesus appears before the highest religious authority in the country that Peter too is on trial . . . before a servant girl and those around her. He then denies Jesus because he has not taken seriously the warning of 14.27 or the advice of the Master, addressed to each disciple, to deny himself (8.34). The irony reaches its climax at v.71: 'but he began to curse and swear: "I do not know the man of whom you are speaking."' The lie made under oath by the disciple hides a profound truth: in fact Peter truly does not know Jesus.

Humour

Irony is invariably built on a contradiction between two levels. If we take the example of Peter denying Jesus (Mark 14.71), Peter is lying in the first degree when he affirms that he does not know Jesus, but this first degree is subtly contradicted by a second level (to abandon the master is in effect not to know him). It would be out of place to argue that this contradiction generates a comic effect. To speak of humour, the discord must be funny.

We have to turn to the attractive story of Jonah if we want a masterpiece of biblical humour. Jonah is so different from the traditional prophets that he is irritated at the success of his preaching: 'Jonah began to go into the city, going a day's journey. And he cried, "Yet forty days, and Nineveh shall be overthrown!" And the people of Nineveh believed God' (3.4–5); and before God's change of mind when he goes back on his decision to punish Nineveh, 'it displeased Jonah exceedingly, and he was angry' (4.1). The comic effect is very marked in this scene, in which God is to speak to his prophet through. . . a plant, the famous gourd (4.6–11).

However, we do not have to wait for Jonah 4 for the comic effect to appear. The whole narrative is built on a collection of scenes which parody classic scenarios: (a) The reluctance of the prophet when he receives the call from the Lord (the effect of parody is evident if one compares it with Ex.4.10; Judg.6.15; Ezra 6.5; Jer.1.6); (b) the behaviour of the sailors during the storm (compare Isa.44.15–17); (c) the psalm of thanksgiving spoken by Jonah in the belly of the fish (compare Ps.130); (d) the reversal of the classic scene in which the prophet sees himself rejected by the king (compare Ex.5.1–11; I Kings 22.13–28); (e) the lamentations of the rejected or desperate prophet (see Num.11.10–15; Jer.20.7–8; I Kings 19.4).

Let us dwell on the fourth scene with its parody: Jonah 3. The reader familiar with the Old Testament will remember the scenes in which the prophet is rejected by the king: Moses before Pharaoh, Micaiah before Ahab, Isaiah before Manasseh, Jeremiah before Zedekiah. Each time, the word of the prophet is transmitted with passion, his message is rejected, and the punishment that has been announced takes place. In Jonah 3, the opposite happens: the prophet pronounces only one phrase, dispassionately; he does not mention any crime committed by the king or by the city, and does not describe the imminent punishment. Now this unusual preaching has a staggering effect: 'By the decree of the king and his nobles: Let neither man nor beast, herd nor flock, taste anything; let them not feed, or drink water, but let man and beast be covered with sackcloth, and let them cry mightily to God' (vv.7–8). Not only is the stereotyped scenario of prophet versus king reversed, but it is taken to extremes: even the animals are associated with the repentance which the king imposes on his subjects.

Why is humour so cultivated in the book of Jonah? The smile asked of the reader hides an eminently theological view on the part of the narrator. The image of God presented in this story, a God who repents of his intention to punish Nineveh, overthrows the traditional religious schemes. As often, the humour serves to put in question the image of a God who is the enemy of the pagans and the protector of his people. The story of Jonah cannot but blunt national pride and the defensive reflexes of popular faith: 'All the laws are thwarted here: *theological laws* because it is the pagans who believe in God better, and in a God who retracts and repents; *psychological and homiletic laws* in which the

THE HUMOUR IN JONAH

most barbarous of people convert *en bloc*, while the good believers accuse God, preferring death to the success of their preaching; *natural laws* with the sudden storms, a curious fish, and soon an amazing gourd... Nothing is normal in this book: everything is abnormal: Jonah, the storm, the fish, the Ninevites, the gourd, the worm, the prayer and even... God! Above all God! Everything and everyone are upside down' (A.Maillot, *Jonas, ou les Farces de Dieu*, 64).

Check your knowledge

- What is the role of the misunderstanding in the narrative of the healing of the paralysed man at Capernaum according to Matt.9.3?
- How does the narrative of the pursuit of Jacob by Laban (Gen.31.17–42) play on irony, indeed humour?

Polysemy

With polysemy, narratology puts its finger on an original effect of narrative rhetoric: deliberate imprecision. Polysemy signifies a plurality of meaning. In English, the word 'rule' (which can mean a regulation, an act of government and a school instrument) is polysemic. Semiology studies how, in the operation of reading, words see their equivocal nature reduced by being grasped in a network of signifiers. To be effective, does not communication require a maximal precision which avoids double meanings?

Now polysemy in particular can be sought for its effect of imprecision or its ambivalence. That is largely the case in poetry. It is also the case in narrativity. In biblical narration the exact sense of a particular term still escapes philology: that is the case with Jonah's plant (Jonah 4.6–11), which the translators call a 'gourd' because they do not know precisely what it was. But for other formulations there are no indications which allow us to reduce the polysemy. If the absence of markers for meaning is asserted, we have to ask whether the polysemy was not sought by the narrator.

The author of Luke-Acts is a specialist in this type of deliberate indecision. His redaction of the declaration of the centurion at the foot of the cross is bizarre. Where Mark wrote, 'Truly this man was Son of God' (15.39), Luke edits it to 'Surely this was a just man' (23.47). But what is the sense of 'just' here? There are two possibilities: this man is 'innocent' or this man is 'a just man'. The legal sense of innocence is supported in the context by the declarations of innocence made by Pilate (23.4,13,22). The theological meaning of the just sufferer is called for by the presence, in the book of Acts, of the appellation 'the Just' to designate Jesus (Acts 3.14; 7.52; 22.14). The Greek allows both. So? One way out of this dilemma is to think that the author was aware of the polysemy and did not want to reduce it. Immediately, the potential of the significance of the cross remains largely open.

We realize what prudence is required before making statements about the effect of polysemy. We would suggest to readers that they try out their shrewdness by reading Luke 2.49 in Greek (must Jesus be 'in my Father's house' or 'about my Father's business'?), Acts 17.22 (are the Athenians

---

FROM THE NARRATOR TO THE FOCALIZER

The Second Gospel is very fond of polyvalent formulations. In the controversy with the scribes on the question of the son of David (Mark 12.35–37), Jesus' argument ends like this: 'David himself calls him Lord, so how is he his son?' Jesus' question indicates an ambiguity: is it aimed at rejecting the idea of the Davidic descent of the Messiah which was current in the first century? Or on the contrary does it maintain this conception, but in a different figurative sense?

In Mark 12.17, replying to his adversaries who are trying to trap him, Jesus declares: 'Render to Caesar that which is Caesar's and to God that which is God's.' When we know the range of interpretations to which this phrase has given rise in the history of exegesis we can only recognize the profound ambiguity of the formula, or rather its polysemy, since it opens up a multiplicity of leads. We are terribly short of foundations for specifying what belongs to the first domain (that of Caesar) and what belongs to the second (God). The polysemy here has an evident rhetorical function: in such a blunt response, which consequently is so clear at first sight, the imprecision is aimed at safeguarding the necessary space for each person to make a completely free ethical decision. If the relative clarity prevents those who contradict Jesus from continuing to question him, the lack of precision intended hinders any return to a rule which applies to every situation. An appeal is made to everyone's reflection.

Polysemy also has a disconcerting effect in Mark's finale: 'And they said nothing to anyone, for they were afraid' (16.8). How are we to interpret the silence of the women and their fear? Are these words charged with a positive sense (respect, fear of God) or do they have a negative connotation (cowardice, an inability to face things)? Is this silence of the women definitive or provisional? If it is definitive, where does the narrative come from which has been made of it?

Robert M.Fowler is one of the ardent defenders of indecision in the Markan text: 'Unlike Matthew or Luke, Mark is comfortable with telling a story rich in ambiguity: he likes to offer puzzles for the reader to solve. In fact the Gospels of Matthew and Luke may represent the earliest evidence we have of people who have responded to the challenge of the puzzles in Mark by retelling Mark's story with the ambiguities clarified and the ironies dissolved' (*Let the Reader Understand*, 17).

POLYSEMY: DUCK OR RABBIT

very religious or very superstitious?), and Acts 27.20–44 (does 'save' denote saving from shipwreck or salvation?).

Rabbinic exegesis has always shown great sensitivity to polysemy in its reading of texts. Here we shall mention only two crucial passages in the Old Testament in which the diversity of translations proposed indicates less a lack of skill on the part of the translators than the wealth of the semantic potential, Ex.3.14 and Deut 6.4b. The first text answers Moses' question about the identity of the God who is sending him. How do we translate it: 'I am he who is?', or 'I am who I am?', or even 'I am who I will be' (I am with you in the way that you see)? The second passage opens the confession of Israel's faith. Here are four possible translations: 1. The Lord, the Lord alone is our God; 2. The Eternal, our God, the Eternal is one; 3. The Lord is our God, (as a) unique Lord; 4. THE LORD our God is the ONE LORD. All these possibilities function together, and none stands out definitively . . . a trace of the mystery and density of the revelation of which the text bears the imprint.

From a narratological point of view, polysemy is interesting by virtue of its effect on the reader, and thus for its pragmatic function. Two effects are essentially sought. Either the ambiguity is removed later in the course of the narrative, or the ambiguity remains. If the readers are constrained to make a choice, they will remember the interpretations which they have dismissed but which remain possible. This virtual openness of meaning enriches their reading, giving them the feeling of a space which is much wider than they had at first imagined. In this setting, the solution adopted to resolve an ambiguity is less important than the interpretative work; it is a work which puts readers before the real dimension of the work which they are interpreting.

Opacity

The last type of 'whispering' (implicit commentary) of the narrative voice is opacity. This narrative technique is absolutely fascinating. Opacity occurs in the narrative the moment the narrator 'sees' something that the characters cannot perceive, or vice versa. In describing the positions of the reader in relation to the characters in the story (> 5.8) we have listed the cases of symmetry (equal position) or dissymetry (an inferior or superior position) in the distribution of information. We are now interested in developing their effects. With opacity there is a real break between the story and the narrative (the level of narrative rhetoric).

Genesis 2: Adam and Eve in the Garden of Eden. At verse 25 the narrator communicates to the narratee an important piece of information: 'And the man and the woman were naked, and they were not ashamed.' The two characters know no shame in being naked: they will learn this later, when they have lost their 'innocence'. But the readers grasp the issue perfectly well. Here is a case in which the opacity is there at the expense of the characters in the story and for the benefit of the reader.

Later, in Gen.18.1–2, there is the opposite phenomenon: 'The Lord appeared to Abraham by the oaks of Mamre as he sat at the door of his tent in the heat of the day. He lifted up his eyes and behold, three men stood in front of him.' What does Abraham see? The narrator speaks of three individuals, but Abraham addresses them by saying, 'My Lord, if I have found favour in your sight. . .' (v.3). Readers have some difficulty in making sense of this obscure designation of God: the transition from v.1 (the Lord) to v.2 ('three men') remains opaque to them. This oblique reference is an invitation to go deeper, to try to grasp it better. Abraham seems to understand immediately something which escapes

---

DEFINITIONS

Implicit commentary: the effect of a meaning which can be imputed to the narrator and is not set down in an explicit statement, perceptible in the action of the plot or in the description of the action of the characters.

Types of implicit commentary

Intertextuality: a phenomenon by which a text refers to other texts by quotation, allusion or echo.

Mirror story (or mise en abyme): reflection on the main narrative integral to the story, through a narrative enclave which functions as a miniaturized summary of the main narrative.

Paradox: construction of the plot showing a linking of facts which goes against common sense.

Misunderstanding: failure of communication between the characters of the story, by which the reader is not fooled.

Symbolism: the effect of meaning by which a motif in the story bears a wider significance, without this being spelt out by the narrative.

Irony: a mode of discourse by which the narrator sets out to suggest a sense opposite to that which he attributes to the characters of the story. The irony can subvert the sense of a discourse (verbal irony) or a situation (dramatic or situational irony).

Polysemy: a plurality of meanings attached to a term or an expression.

Opacity: withholding information to the detriment of the reader or a character in the story.

---

the reader. In a way, the reader is put at a disadvantage, a victim of the opacity of the narrative.

The veil of opacity is particularly evident in Mark 14.36–38. This is the narrative of the vigil in Gethsemane, at the time of the passion. Jesus has taken Peter, James and John with him to ask them to remain in a place and to keep watch. He himself has gone on a little further to pray. The narratee is then told the prayer of Jesus (the only one communicated to him throughout the Gospel!): 'Abba, Father, all things are possible for you, remove this cup from me...' Then Jesus gets up, goes back to the three disciples and finds them asleep.

We can draw two conclusions: first, a veil of opacity has fallen on the characters, while the narratee benefits from the information given; secondly, the narratee himself is informed only afterwards of the sleep into which the disciples have fallen, so that he realizes, retrospectively, that he has been the only companion to keep awake with Jesus at Gethsemane. The moment of transparency in the narrative rhetoric proves a moment of opacity in the story. Now this moment is particularly significant, since the reader discovers (v.36) the way in which

Jesus addresses his Father ('Abba'), his absolute trust in him ('all things are possible for you'), the intensity of his agony ('take this cup from me'), and at the same time his total submission to the divine will ('not what I will, but what you will'). This prayer illuminates the whole passion, conferring on it a sense of abandonment which is fully accepted by Jesus from his Father. The characters in the story are excluded from all this. The disequilibrium of the sources of information is such that the narratee is the only one to be present at the whole of the scene.

Check your knowledge

- Find the humour in the way in which the demoniac of Gerasa is liberated (Mark 5.1–20).
- What is the sense of the claim of the people who ask the prophet Samuel for a king (I Sam.8.19–20)?
- The phenomenon of opacity (in the narratological sense) has its effect in the narrative of I Sam.28 (Saul and the witch of Endor). What is the result for the reader?

We find in Mark 4.10–13 (the reason for the parables) another example of opacity, which is particularly troublesome. Taking note of v.11, which evokes the 'mystery of the kingdom of God' given to the disciples, readers are disconcerted. They would like to discover where and when this mystery has been unveiled to the disciples; they find nothing satisfactory. There is a secret which escapes them, a break in communication in a moment when the history is continuing to unfold. The rest of the narrative raises other questions, to which we shall be returning in the next chapter (> 9.4).

The reader's response

Intertextuality, mirror text, paradox, misunderstanding, symbolism, irony, humour, polysemy, opacity: all these are examples of indirect communication in which we see the importance of what takes place in the reception of the text. The more implicit the message, the more the participation of the reader in the act of reading must be an active one. Where the implicit commentary broadens out, the narrative is in fact firmly 'reader orientated'. This observation is at the heart of a branch of narrative criticism entirely focussed on the response that the text calls the reader to give, reader-response criticism. We shall now turn our attention to some themes developed by this current, in connection with the role of the reader in the act of reading.

For further reading

M. Bal, *Femmes imaginaires*, Paris: Nizet 1986, 166–80 (*mise en abyme*).

R. A. Culpepper, *Anatomy of the Fourth Gospel*, Philadelphia: Fortress Press 1983, 149–202 (implicit commentaries in the Fourth Gospel).

G. Genette, *Figures III*, Paris: Editions du Seuil 1972, 225–67 (theorization of the narrative 'voice').

N. Piégay-Gros, *Introduction à l'intertextualité*, Paris: Dunod 1996 (manual on intertextuality).

9

The role of the text and the role of the reader

Like tennis, reading takes two to play. And for the game to be played well, both the sides must have talent. Far from being reduced to a passive registration, reading is a magic which brings the text to life – for the text is dead unless it is looked at by the reader who gives it life by deciphering it. But at the same time, if the reader's course through it has not been helped and guided by the narrator, the reading goes wrong, laboriously seeking its way in the labyrinth of words.

For the reading to work, it is therefore important for each to keep to their role: the text helps the readers to go through it by marking out their route, and in return the readers give life to the text, which is an incomplete entity.

9.1 The incompleteness of the text

In his *Lector in fabula*, Umberto Eco says that the text is 'a lazy (or economic) mechanism which lives on the surplus value of the meaning introduced by the receiver' (66–67). A literary work is in fact always sent out to a readership capable of reading it: to arrive at its destination the text needs the participation of the reader. 'A text needs someone to help it to function,' Eco goes on to say; 'a text is sent out for someone capable of actualizing it' (67).

Thus the text is a lazy machine which delegates part of its work to the reader. By definition the textual universe is incomplete. What is called the

IT TAKES TWO TO READ

121

aesthetic effect of the text is this appeal by the text to be received. Every text bears in itself a hope for a reader; or, to put it differently, a reader is always implicit in the text. Jean Delorme remarks that the 'narrative has its way of attracting a subject to listen to it. . . Without addressing him, it captures his faculties and puts them into action' (*Au risque de la parole*, 157). Without the interpretative co-operation of the reader the text is a storehouse from which nothing will extract the treasures. There's the fatal word: for there to be reading, and thus a production of meaning, *the active co-operation of the reader* is needed. There is no magic of reading without an interaction between the text and its recipient.

The paradox of reading

How is the narrator going to solicit this interaction, since by definition the text is a differentiated communication? In space and time narrator and narratee are separated: they are not in each other's presence (spatial distance); on the other hand there is always a time-lag between the reader's response to the appeal of the text and the point of writing, and this time-lag (of several minutes or several centuries) constitutes the chronological distance.

Hence the paradox of reading, which must bow to the text without the leisure to obtain supplementary information from the author. But at the same time, no law tells the reader how to read. Readers enjoy immense freedom, since within the limits assigned to them by the writing they can make comparisons, connections, links between the elements of the texts which the author has not necessarily foreseen. Without always being aware of it, every reader benefits from this paradox in the ordinary practice of reading, investing in the text effects of unexpected meanings, coming from outside the text or prompted by the text.

This interplay of constraint and freedom first of all raises the problem of the limits of interpretation: does a text authorize every reading? What is the link, say, between a first meaning of the text envisaged by the narrator and the latent meanings exploited to the taste and opinions of the reader? Can one, must one, regulate the reading? Here we have chosen to touch on one aspect of the problem: the programming of the reading by the text. The other question, that of the limits of interpretation, will be the subject of the next chapter (>10.2).

An unfinished text

As we have said, the text needs a co-operative reader, i.e. a reader 'capable of co-operating with the textual actualization as he, the author, thinks fit and also capable of acting interpretatively as the author has acted generatively' (U. Eco, *Lector in fabula*, 71). The talent of delivering a text symmetrically calls for the talent of a midwife, and the reader is assigned this role.

The incompleteness of the text results from a simple observation: the text does not say everything; to aim at exhaustiveness in a description would be tedious. This partial aspect is even more true in the biblical narratives. When the narrative builds a world (with its actions and characters) it is impossible for it to say everything about this world; it mentions features and otherwise asks the reader to collaborate by filling in the empty spaces.

Vincent Jouve (*La Lecture*, 44–6) lists four registers on which the reader is active: the probable, the logic of the actions, symbolic language, and the general significance of the work.

1. Since the narrator cannot and does not want to say everything, the readers complete the narrative in their imaginations by virtue of what seems to them to be **probable**. 'A Pharisee invited (Jesus) to eat with him; he went into the Pharisee's house and sat at table. A woman of the town came who was a sinner' (Luke 7.36–37a). Nothing is said about who was at the table, how Jesus was dressed, what the woman looked like, the number and the reactions of the guests. . . The few features selected are enough for the narrator, who relies on the culture and imagination of the reader to finish the picture. Eco, once again, lays down the following rule: everything that

the text does not describe explicitly as being different from the reality that the reader knows is to be completed in terms of the laws and situations of his world (*Six Walks in the Fictional Woods*, 83). It is by virtue of this practice of completion, we might say in passing, that the filming of a narrative can seem reductive; while it is possible to reproduce the facts and dialogues, the film version of an atmosphere or a character will never coincide with the reader's imagination.

2. If the narrator omits the description of minor actions, the readers themselves reconstruct **the logic of the actions**. There is no need to spell out that to enter a house it is necessary to find the entrance, go through the door and take several steps inside: 'Jesus entered' is sufficient description. Similarly with this phrase in II Sam.12.15–16a: 'And the Lord struck the child that Uriah's wife bore to David, and he became sick. David therefore besought God for the child.' From God's decision to David's prayer, the reader automatically infers links absent in the sequence of actions. However, the logic of actions has its limits in the distance which can open up between the customs of the world of the narrative (for the Bible, Israel or ancient Greece) and the world of the reader: sometimes, for want of sufficient historical information, the reader goes against the meaning.

3. To perceive **the symbolic dimension** of the language is also a performance on the part of the reader, since this dimension relates to the implicit commentary (> 8.2). The symbol comes under the jurisdiction of what is not said. Reading consists in basing oneself both on what the text says and what it suggests.

4. Without the narrator needing to remind them, the readers put each episode read within **the general significance of the work** or, if you like, within the plot of the main narrative, which they progressively elaborate. When David launches his troops against the Philistines or when Paul and his companions go from one city to another, the reader does not expect a summary of military strategy or a travel description: the issue is to be sought rather in the divine guidance of the story. Furthermore the biblical authors can incite the readers to discern the general significance of the main narrative by summaries or repetitive formulae. The author of the books of Kings, for example, hammers home his judgment on the impious kings (and associates the reader with it) by repeating a simple formula: 'He did what was evil in the eyes of the Lord' (II Kings 15.9,28; 17.2; 21.2,20; 23.32). The author of the Acts of the Apostles recalls at regular intervals that the scarlet thread of his narrative is the irrepressible growth of the church (2.41,47b; 5.14; 6.7; 9.31; 11.21; 12.24, etc.).

The interaction between text and reader

The interaction between the text and its reader, which is the co-operation between narrator and narratee spoken of above, takes several forms which should not be confused. On a first level come the measures taken by the narrator to programme the reader's course (9.2). At a second level it is necessary to note the competence of the reader to which the narrator appeals (9.3). But the interactive relationship can go further, to the point of the means deployed by the narrator to construct a competence or position with the reader: it is the third level of interactivity which is perceptible (9.4).

9.2 The programming of the reading

Without explicitly saying so, the text suggests to its readers a certain number of conventions which make a kind of reading contract with them. This is the famous *reading* pact.

The affiliation of the narrative to a specific literary genre leads it to be placed within the literary culture of the time; it also has the effect of indicating to the reader how it must be read. For in doing this it assumes the constraints and permissions of the genre: it is subject to more or less clear norms which

READERS IN ALL THEIR STATES

Narratologists are not agreed on the status of the implied reader. Schematically, three directions are explored in research: a reconstructive approach, a pragmatic approach and an interactive approach.

The *reconstructive approach*: detaching the image of the reader inscribed in the work makes it possible to reconstruct the view the author has of his readership (M.Corti; S.Chatman). Following this perspective, R.A.Culpepper (*Anatomy of the Fourth Gospel*) has collected right through the Fourth Gospel all the traits attributable to the implicit reader initially envisaged by the text: knowledge of the scriptures, not belonging to Judaism, ignorance of the geography of Palestine and Jewish rites, familiarity with the tradition of Jesus, etc. He arrives at a representation of the readership inherent in the text without saying whether this image coincides with the real readers of the Gospel in the first century.

The *pragmatic approach*: Umberto Eco defines under the label 'model reader' a 'set of textual instructions, displayed by the text's linear manifestation precisely as a set of sentences or other signals' (*Six Walks in the Fictional Woods*, 15f.). According to Eco, the author programmes the reading of his text by giving directives in order to be understood (information, explanations, anticipated announcements, etc.): this collection of instructions inscribes in the text the profile of the reader expected by the text. This is a 'model reader capable of co-operating in actualizing the text in the way in which he, the author, thought, and capable of acting interpretatively' (*Lector in fabula*, 71). Eco's model reader is thus a programmed receiver.

The *interactive approach*: unlike U.Eco, W.Iser emphasizes that the role of the reader is not identical with the marks of the potential reader inscribed in the text. There is tension between the real reader and the role in which the text suggests he should immerse himself, so that the implicit reader coincides with the best decipherment of the text desired by the author. 'The implicit reader is not the abstraction of a real reader. He is rather the condition of a tension which the reader experiences in accepting this role' (*L'Acte de lecture*, 73). Or in the words of W.Booth: 'The author sketches out an image of himself and an image of his reader. He constructs his reader as a second self, and the best readings are those in which the selves created, the author and the reader, are capable of coming in perfect accord' (*The Rhetoric of Fiction*, 138).

Within the nebula of readings inspired by narratology, each is defined by the position which it attaches to the reader in relationship to the text. The deconstructionism inspired by Derrida puts the reader above the text; it is for him to disengage the infinity of possible meanings from the text. The reader in reader-response criticism is placed *in front of* the text; he pilots the reading, but in interaction with the text (R.M.Fowler; W.Iser). Narrative criticism in the strict sense detects the image of the reader *in* the text, traced in intaglio by the representation that the text makes of itself and the signals that it addresses to him (U. Eco).

This book takes account of the two latter positions. To illuminate the debate between Eco and Iser, let us spell out the issue. The debate turns on the fact that the former bases himself on the text, while the latter's definition comes from the process of reading. Eco emphasizes the inscription, directly in the text, of the programme of co-operation between the author and the reader with a view to the reading (but the frontier between the particular reading of a reader and that of the model reader, in other words the difference between critical interpretation and 'co-operative interpretation', remains fluid). Iser, considering that the reading unfolds *from* the text and not *in* the text, puts his implied reader between the text and the real reader – where the production of meaning operates. Does one one day become an implied reader, according to Iser's definition? No, for the figure of the implicit reader recapitulates all the possible effects of the text.

For the definitions of the reader see:

U.Eco, *Lector in fabula*, Paris: Grasset 1985, especially 64–111.

G.Genette, *Nouveau discours du récit*, Paris: Editions du Seuil 1983, 93–107.

W.Iser, *L'Acte de lecture: théorie de l'effet esthétique*, Brussels: Mardaga 1985; *Der implizite Leser*, Munich: Fink 1994.

V.Jouve, *La Lecture*, Paris: Hachette 1993, 23–41 (a good synthesis).

are going to codify its reception. Just as one would not take umbrage at miraculous episodes in fairy stories (one even expects them), whereas they would be shocking in a modern historical chronicle, similarly the presence of supernatural interventions and moral lessons do not surprise the readers of the great Jewish historical works (the Deuteronomistic history) or Christian historical works (the book of Acts). On the other hand, one would not expect from ancient historians the documentary view that one demands from history books today; so it is important to inform oneself of the tacit reading contract which is implied by the borrowing of a literary genre of the age.

However, the reading pact is linked more precisely with two privileged textual locations: what Gérard Genette calls the *peritext* and the *incipits*.

The peritext

The *peritext* is what *surrounds* the text. What Genette (*Paratexts,*) proposes to call by this name is every-thing that relates to the strategy of the preface, everything that is put before the narrative proper with a view to orientating its reading: preface, introduction, foreword, prologue. In short, the peritext denotes every prior form of warning the reader. It is an instrument at the disposition of the narrator to indicate why and how one must read.

The peritext is to be distinguished from the *epitext*, where Genette suggests one puts the broader periphery of the text which prepares for and governs its consumption: commentary on the text, illustrations, critical studies, etc. Unlike the peritext, the epitext does not touch the text physically; a commentary on the text presented as a preface (or epilogue) is transformed into peritext. Epitext and peritext together constitute what Genette calls the *paratext*, i.e. everything that 'makes the text present, to safeguard its presence to the world, its reception and its consumption'.

We immediately see how useful these categories are when we find ourselves confronted with the preface of Luke-Acts (Luke 1.1–4, taken up in Acts

THE PERITEXT: THE WORK PUT IN CONTEXT

1.1–2) or the book of Revelation (1.1–3), the prologue of the Fourth Gospel (John 1.1–18) or the infancy narratives in the Gospels (Matt.1–2; Luke 1.5–2.52). The function of these sequences read as peritext is not simply to introduce the narrative, as is often said; it is to fix the status of the narrative by dictating the norms of the reading pact. These prefaces overhang the text, providing an indispensable key to reading for anyone who wants to understand the text in keeping with the intention of the one who conceived it. Like the key signature at the beginning of a piece of music, they fix a tonality for the whole piece.

Thus Luke 1.1–4 confers on Luke's work a status of historical chronicle (in the Graeco-Roman sense) and not of an eyewitness account; the author of the work to Theophilus is positioning himself as a historian and indicating the parameters (careful information and ordering of the narrative) which his work obeys. The prologue of the Fourth Gospel (John 1.1–18) discerns in the Jesus whose story the narrative will unfold the theological dignity of the pre-existing Logos (the incarnate emanation of the eternal Word of God). Matthew 1–2 and Luke 1–2 prefigure the whole Gospel, attaching the fulfilment of the promises of scripture in the coming of the child-God, but announcing the drama that is to be played out by God and Israel around Jesus.

In the case of John 1, Matt.1–2 and Luke 1–2, the effect is intensified by a surplus of knowledge given to the reader about the characters in the story which will follow; the peritext thus constructs a superior position for the reader (> 5.8) in the face of the whole network of characters in the Gospel outside Jesus.

The incipit

Everyone knows how important the first words exchanged are in an encounter between two people. The same goes for the first phrases of a text: it is through these that the author makes contact with his reader. So the beginning is the first step in the deliberate production of meaning. The Latin name *incipit* (= it begins) has been kept for these beginnings of text. 'Once upon a time' is a typical *incipit* which by the use of the imperfect relating to an indeterminate past helps the reader's or hearer's imagination to blossom. The *incipit* fixes a kind of setting for the story by establishing a protocol of reading; but what is signified explicitly in the peritext remains implicit here, namely that the first phrases of the text announce the narrator's intention without his explaining himself (unlike Luke 1.1–4).

Let's look closely at the beginning of beginnings, i.e. how the first book of the Bible begins. The narrative of Genesis 1 starts with the words 'In the beginning, God created heaven and earth' (a better translation would be: 'At the beginning of the creation by God of heaven and earth'). Genesis 1.1 prepares the reader admirably to enter the world of the creation narrative, but also the biblical narrative as a whole. For the text speaks of beginning, hence the reader knows that the narrative is second, that it comes after the event; no one can be present at the beginning of things. The rabbis emphasize this fact by commenting that the first word of the Bible, *bereshit* (in the beginning), begins not with the first but with the second letter of the Hebrew alphabet, *beth*. So the first verse of the Bible resolutely makes God and his creative action initiate everything (the expression 'heaven and earth' is a phrase denoting totality). God is the one who imposes limits and contracts on all humankind in the stories of the beginnings (Gen.1–11), and God is the one who will guide the particular history of the Hebrew people from Genesis 12. The next verse (Gen.1.2) functions as a reading pact for the first creation narrative, describing the act of creation as the organization of chaos by God. So the creation is motivated solely by the will of God. Chaos has no other origin that could be explained by mythology: the creative word, under the form of an order, resounds without there yet being any partner to receive it. Thus in two verses the incipit of Genesis has posited God as the absolute beginning and puts creation, including human beings, in a necessary relationship to him.

DEFINITIONS

Reading pact: the totality of the conventions by which the narrator programmes the reception of the text by the reader and circumscribes the act of reading. The reading pact is made explicitly through the peritext and implicitly through the literary genre of the narrative.

Paratext: the totality of statements which surround a text and condition its reading: the paratext is composed of the peritext and the epitext.

Peritext: statements immediately preceding or following the text which condition its reading (title, preface, prologue, conclusion).

Epitext: statements constructing a setting in which the text is communicated and which prepare for reading it, while being separate from it (commentary, summary, blurb, etc.): the epitext can come from either the author or the publisher.

Incipit: the statement with which a text begins and which functions as a protocol for reading addressed to the reader.

Waymarks for reading

We have seen how the reading pact (conventions of a literary kind, peritext) sets out to channel the reception of the narrative among its readers. Now the programming of the reading does not stop at the fixing of a setting; the narrator continually provides the text with signals which orientate readers in their work of decipherment. Psycholinguistic studies have shown how far the presence (or absence) of these signals orientates (or disorientates) the cognitive representation of the text in the memory. At the linguistic level, the way in which conjunctions like *but, and, however, or*, etc. function in cognitive guidance is crucial; remove them from the text and the reading goes astray. Here we shall be more interested in narrative waymarks.

The most obvious indications are the signals of **narrative structuring**. Here are two examples among many: the author of the books of Kings punctuates his royal chronicles with the same formula: 'Is it not written in the book of the chronicles of the kings of Israel?' (I Kings 14.19,29; 15.7,23; 16.5, 14, 20, 27; 22.39, 46; II Kings 10.34; 13.8, 12; 14.15, 18, 28; 15.36; 16.19; 20.20; 21.17,25); the evangelist Matthew ends Jesus' five discourses with an identical refrain: 'When Jesus had finished these words' (7.28; 11.1; 13.53; 19.1; 26.1). The indications which introduce an episode or move characters from one episode to another are to be put in the same category.

Another waymark is **redundancy**. The repetition of an event or a formula allows readers to weave links, to bring things together, to remind themselves of the general line of the work. We spoke earlier (> 7.1) about the refrains relating to growth which punctuate the narrative in Acts (2.47b: 'And the Lord added to their number day by day those who were being saved'); here the redundancy helps towards the general aim of the work, which is to explain the success of Christianity in the world. This procedure is already known from the Old Testament. We need only recall the disillusioned statement of Koheleth, 'all is vanity' (1.2, 14; 2.1, 11, 15, 17, 19, 23, 26, etc.), which gives rhythm to his reflection on the impossible task of the necessary wisdom.

A variant of redundancy is **syncrisis**. This procedure takes its name from Graeco-Roman rhetoric: it consists in putting the activity of several characters in parallel, with a view either to comparing them or to marking the continuity from one to the other. In the New Testament Luke is the champion of *syncrisis*: he shows this when he relates in very similar

SYNCRISIS: AN ECHO PHENOMENON

The three healings of a paralysed man; Jesus, Peter and John, Paul

Luke 5.18–25

And behold, men were bringing on a bed a man who was paralysed, and they sought to bring him in and lay him before Jesus; but finding no way to bring him in, because of the crowd, they went up on the roof and let him down with his bed through the tiles into the midst before Jesus. And when he saw their faith he said, 'Man, your sins are forgiven you.' And the scribes and the Pharisees began to question, saying, 'Who is this that speaks blasphemies? Who can forgive sins but God only?' When Jesus perceived their questionings, he answered them, 'Why do you question in your hearts? Which is easier, to say, "Your sins are forgiven you", or to say, "Rise and walk?" But that you may know that the Son of man has authority on earth to forgive sins' – he said to the man who was paralysed – 'I say to you, rise, take up your bed and go home.' And immediately he rose before them, and took up that on which he lay, and went home, glorifying God.

Acts 3.1–8

Now Peter and John were going up to the temple at the hour of prayer, the ninth hour. And a man lame from birth was being carried whom they laid daily at that gate of the temple which is called Beautiful to ask alms of those who entered the temple. Seeing Peter and John about to go into the temple, he asked for alms. And Peter directed his gaze at him, with John, and said, 'Look at us.' And he fixed his attention upon them, expecting to receive something from them. But Peter said, 'I have no silver and gold, but I give you what I have; in the name of Jesus Christ of Nazareth, walk.' And he took him by the right hand and raised him up; and immediately his feet and ankles were made strong. And leaping up he stood and walked and entered the temple with them, walking and leaping and praising God.

Acts 14.8–10

Now at Lystra there was a man sitting, who could not use his feet; he was a cripple from birth, who had never walked. He listened to Paul speaking; and Paul, looking intently at him and seeing that he had faith to be made well, said in a loud voice, 'Stand upright on your feet.' And he sprang up and walked. And when the crowds saw what Paul had done, they lifted up their voices, saying in Lycaonian, 'The gods have come down to us in the likeness of men.'

terms the healing of a sick man by Jesus, by Peter and by Paul (see the box), or when he attributes the resurrection of a dead person to Jesus, then to Peter and then to Paul (Luke 8.49–56; Acts 9.36–43; 20.7–12). The intention of marking the continuity from the Gospel of Luke to the book of Acts is manifest. The narrator counts on the memory of his reader and calls for it by the use of repetitive formulae from one narrative to another; he implicitly induces the effect of a repetition of the miracles of Jesus through the apostles, and the readers see themselves confirmed in this opinion by Peter's declaration about the healing of the sick man at the beautiful gate: 'Men of Israel, why do you wonder at this, or why do you stare at us, as though by our own power of piety we had made him walk? His name, by faith in his name, has made this man strong whom you see and know; and the faith

LUKE 5   ACTS 3   ACTS 14

which is through Jesus has given this man perfect health. . .' (Acts 3.12b,16). So the discourse spells out and confirms what the narrative procedure of *syncrisis* has set in place: the healing by the apostles is repeating the healing action of Jesus.

The procedure of *syncrisis* is not unknown in the Hebrew Bible; after the two almost identical narratives relating how to save his life the patriarch Abraham passes off his wife as his sister (Gen. 12.10–20; 20), Genesis 26 tells the same story but attributes it to Isaac (26.1–11).

The phenomenon of **intertextuality**, already touched on in the framework of the implicit commentary (> 8.2), can also be put among the signals for orientating reading. The motive is identical to that in syncrisis: the use of formulae taken from the Septuagint (the Greek translation of the Old Testament) by the New Testament writers appeals to the memory of the readers and guides their interpretation with reference to prototypical figures. There is no doubt that the first readers of the Gospels and Acts was much more at ease in finding these references than today's readers, if only by virtue of their knowledge of the Greek translation of the Old Testament.

The gaps in the text

So far, the programming of the reading has been described as an appeal to the readers to base their understanding of the text on the indications of convergence, difference, distribution or hierarchy of sequences. But over against these places of certainty there are places of uncertainty where readers must orientate their reading with the help of two leads, one of which is legible and one illegible.

What do we have here? As we have seen, a narrator can decide to guide the reading with the help of particular signals. But he can also ask for the co-operation of the reader by leaving spaces which are indeterminate: he chooses elements that he leaves to the creativity of the reader. The deliberate absence of specifics is a very sure way of programming the effect of a narrative. The text speaks as much by what it does not say as what it does say.

There are two ways of looking at a tree: seeing its

DEFINITIONS

Syncrisis: a rhetorical procedure consisting of putting in parallel two characters or two situations in the narrative with a view to comparing them: *syncrisis* sets up an interplay in which while being continuous they go beyond each other.

Gaps in the text: a technique by which the narrator deprives the reader of important information enjoyed, for example, by the characters of the story. This type of lacuna, consisting in the omission of a constitutive part of the narration (for example, the systematic concealment of a character) is called *paralipsis*.

foliage or seeing the holes left by its leaves. The painter Louis Soutter favoured the latter, thus taking up Chinese painting, in which the balance of gaps is more important than the elements which are drawn. Walter Iser has studied this phenomenon which he calls the 'gaps' in the text.

For example, the narrative of the Flood does not tell us the provenance of the animals needed for the holocaust offered by Noah after coming out of the ark (Gen.8.20–21); the narrator puts the importance of the cult above coherence with 6.19–20. Or in the episode of the selling of Joseph to the Midianites (Gen.37), we are not told of any reaction on the part of the brother who is sold. Joseph is an innocent and mute victim of the violence of his brothers. That adds to the offensiveness of the situation and leads the reader to put into words the injustice done to him. At the end of the cycle (Gen.45) Joseph will give the interpretation of his story, while his brothers no longer have a say... but the reader knows

that the words of the brothers would not justify their action.

In an extreme case the narrator can aim at leading the reader astray. In the parable of the workers at the eleventh hour, the owner of the vineyard engages the workers at different hours, promising them 'what is right' (Matt.20.4); they conclude (and the reader with them) that the wages will be proportionate to the duration of the work. The parable functions at a narrative level on this 'place of uncertainty', which will serve to put in crisis the notion of justice that the reader shares with the characters of the story (20.13–15).

9.3 The competences of the reader

All that has been said about reading programmed by the text could suggest that with the final full stop given by the author to his work, the reception of the text has already been played out. Does one read it under constraint? Is the act of reading the unsur-

THE GAPS IN THE TEXT

Check your knowledge

- In what way does the *incipit* of the First Gospel situate the story of Jesus which is to follow?
- How do the books of Kings use the procedure of *syncrisis* to show that Elisha is the worthy successor to Elijah (cf. I Kings 17; II Kings 4)?
- Each of the three stories of calls in Luke 8.57–62 omits to relate something. What? What sense does this produce?

prising unfolding of a planned scenario? The simple fact that at any moment readers can give up their reading and close the book shows their freedom. What was said earlier about the effects of unexpected meaning evoked by the imagination of the readers confirms that they can ask questions about the narrative outside the ways foreseen by the author.

Once again, the term co-operation deserves to be taken completely seriously. The text plays with competences of reading which it does not master but presupposes in the readers, and the result of which escapes it, at least in part. Umberto Eco has used several metaphors to explain this interaction. He compares the act of reading to a walk in the woods at which each fork in the path calls for a choice of itinerary. He also compares it to a ride on a train (which track to choose) or a chess match (foresee the ploy of the partner, the narrator). Eco thinks of the faculty to anticipate, which with memory makes up the two major competences of readers.

Predicting in reading

To anticipate what comes next in a story is a basic reflex of every reader. The need to understand and predict explains the incessant construction of hypotheses on how the plot will go and what is at stake: this activity of prediction takes the reading forward. If the outcome of the biblical story is not in doubt (God will triumph over evil), the suspense rests on how and why. Constantly anticipating, readers are continually read to validate of invalidate the hypotheses that they make.

Knowing this, the narrator can be ingenious in thwarting the expectations of the reader, rather like a detective story which slips in false clues or ambiguous signs to disorientate the activity of predicting. It's a game, but this game is anything but superficial. When the narrator introduces Hannah as a childless woman, Zacchaeus as a chief tax collector, or Rahab as a prostitute, he induces in the reader a kind of expectation about their behaviour which the narrative is going to work to thwart. By forcing readers to put their pictures in question in this way, the narrator participates in the reconstruc-

---

TO READ IS TO PREDICT

'...A wood is a garden of forking paths. Even where there are not well-trodden paths in a wood, everyone can trace his or her own parh, deciding to go to the left or to the right of a certain tree and making a choice at every tree encountered. In a narrative text, at each instant the reader must make a choice' (U Eco, *Six Walks in the Fictional Woods*, 6).

'To become attentive means making predictions. The model reader is called on to collaborate in the development of the *fabula* by anticipating its successive stages. The reader's anticipation is a portion of the *fabula* which *should* correspond to what he is going to read. Once he has read it, he will see whether or not the text has confirmed his prediction' (U.Eco, *Lector in fabula*, 148).

'In a comparison with chess, a narrative text can resemble both a manual for children and a manual for experts. In the first case, game situations will be offered which are quite obvious (according to a chess encyclopaedia) so that the child has the satisfaction of making successful predicitons; in the second case, game situations will be presented in which the victor has attempted a completely unexpected coup which no scenario has yet recorded, a coup which will go down to posterity for its bravery and novelty, so that the reader feels the pleasure of seeing himself contradicted' (U.Eco, *Lector in fabula*, 153).

---

tion of narrative identity, something which we shall be discussing again later (>10.3).

This process is at work in the book of Jeremiah. The book opens with a narrative about the prophet's call, which assures the prophet that he will fulfil his difficult mission (to proclaim the exile to the people) and gives him signs of this (Jer.1.4–19). The reader, warned by the narrative of the prophet's vocation, easily anticipates the fate which is reserved for him: Jeremiah will end up like the other prophets, notably Hananiah. The reader cannot fail to predict that the narrative will invite him to enter into Jeremiah's inner debate (the Confessions) or that the prophet will end up not being killed but exiled, ironically to Egypt and not to Babylon.

Here is another example of induction. When the evangelist Matthew brings 'Herod the tetrarch' on the scene in chapter 14, the reader immediately remembers another Herod, the father, who in chapter 2 had had the new-born children massacred in the hope of destroying the Messiah. The image of the former Herod, summoned up in the memory, immediately casts its shadow over the killing of John the Baptist by the latter, creating in the narrative a malevolent pole on the side of the Herodian royal family.

And when, having reached the end of the Gospel, the readers of Matthew learn the last words of the risen Christ, 'I will be with you always, to the end of the world' (28.20), their memories should remind them of how these words fit with the prophecy

READING – PREDICTING IS FULL OF UNCERTAINTIES

received by Joseph at the beginning of the narrative: 'Behold, a virgin shall conceive and bear a son, and his name shall be called Emmanuel, which being translated means "God with us"' (1.23). The arch spread between the beginning and the end of Matthew's narration confirms to the reader that the aim of the narrative was to show how, by what actions and by what words, God has manifested himself 'with us' in human history.

The example of Jeremiah and Matthew shows that if reading is predicting, it is also a phenomenon of memory. There is continual coming and going between what is memorized and what is envisaged, between retention (of what is past) and prediction (of what is to come). Reading experiences this movement of goings and comings, but it is not the only one: every learning process follows the same dialectic. As Jean-Michel Adam has put it: in reading 'the cognitive process is a coming and going from the antecedent to the *consequent* which is envisaged and from the *consequent* to the *antecedent* which is reconstructed' (*Le texte narratif*, 29).

So reading is a perpetual movement in which hypotheses are constructed that the narrative confirms or disconfirms, in which facts accumulate in the memory which the advancement of the narrative will use and reconstruct. So the role of memory is fundamental, and refining its function in reading leads to a distinction between a short-term working memory and a long-term memory which stores up the facts of the narrative so far, simplifying them.

Projective logic

The inventory of the reader's competences also includes the faculty to project feelings of sympathy, empathy or antipathy on to the characters in the narrative. Of course this process is begun by the narrator himself (>5.6). Nevertheless, to be moved by the distress of a father or to vibrate to the denunciation of social injustice brings into play in readers a wealth of experiences, convictions and real life which are peculiarly theirs.

Check your knowledge

- How, in the story of the Fall (Gen.3), does the narrator play on the reader's capacity to predict?
- In what sense is the reader of John 3 (the conversation between Jesus and Nicodemus) led to anticipate the sequence of events?

The personal encyclopaedia

Let's end with something which is self-evident. As in every process of communication, the despatcher postulates that the receiver has a stock of knowledge that one can call a personal encyclopaedia. According to Umberto Eco, this linguistic competence ideally comprises a basic dictionary, rules of co-reference (making it possible to identify the 'she' or 'he' who is being spoken of), the faculty to analyse an expression in terms of its context, intertextuality, the deciphering of the stylistic code and a so-called 'ideological competence' (identifying a system of values). Depending on the encyclopaedic competence which he attributes to the implicit reader or which he does not assign him, the narrator will provide his text with commentaries of an explicit kind ('They led him to the place called Golgotha, *which means place of the skull*', Mark 15.22).

Now the reading does not leave the reader's personal encyclopaedia untouched. Not only can it grow (by an addition of information), but above all, reading leads to modifying, confirming or subverting the reader's view of the world by confronting it with that of the narrator. The narrative is the narrative offer of a vision of the world which interrogates the readers when they return to their world. We shall analyse later how this effect of returning in reading functions (>10.1).

In every case evoked so far, the co-operation of the reader is required, on the basis of the competences attributed to him by the narrator. Whether this is trying to programme the reception of the text (peritext or waymarks in reading) or in calling on the reader's competences (anticipation, retention, projection, encyclopaedia), the narrator relies on the faculties of the consumers of the text. Now the interaction between text and reader does not stop there. The narrator can in fact decide to model the competence of the reader as he likes, or to influence the image that the reader has of him. We call this process the construction of the reader by the text.

9.4 The construction of the reader by the text

Here once again we are guided by the intuitions of Umberto Eco. How does the 'lazy mechanism', the text, foresee the intervention of the reader which is indispensable to making it function? To predict that its reader will co-operate 'does not solely signify "hoping" that he exists,' remarks the Italian semiotician. 'It also signifies acting on the text by way of constructing it. So a text is based on a competence but, in addition, it contributes towards producing it' (*Lector in fabula*, 72). Eco's thesis is that to be read, a text does not just presuppose the competence of the reader; it constructs a reader who is competent to read it. Like furniture delivered in kit form, the text not only offers itself to be read, but also gives the readers, to this end, their own way of using it.

The decipherment of the symbolic element in the Fourth Gospel perfectly supports this way of looking at things.

Deciphering the symbolic element in John

The Fourth Gospel abounds in metaphors: I am the light of the world, I am the bread from heaven, the good shepherd, the living water, the vine, behold the lamb of God. . . To be grasped, this process of symbolization, which in John attains an unparalleled frequency and intensity, requires the reader to go beyond the obvious meaning (the bread, the lamb, the vine) to reach the figurative level. Several misunderstandings in the course of the Gospel indicate that not everyone can manage progress towards the full sense: Nicodemus does not understand what being born from above is (John 3.4); the

ONE ALWAYS HAS THE READER IN MIND WHEN WRITING

'When you write, you are thinking of a reader, as the painter, while he paints, is thinking of the viewer who will look at the picture. After making a brush stroke, he takes two or three steps back and studies the effect; he looks at the picture, that is the way the viewer would admire it in proper lighting, when it is hanging on a wall. When a work is finished, a dialogue is established between the text and its readers (the author is excluded), while a work is in progress, the dialogue is double: there is the dialogue between that text and all other previously written texts (books are made only from other books and around other books), and there is the dialogue between the author and his model reader' (U.Eco, *Reflections on The Name of the Rose*, 47).

Samaritan woman expects living water from the well (4.11f.); and the disciples confuse obeying and eating (4.32–34). These repeated failures in communication alert the reader to the risk of incompetence.

Now an attentive observation of the text will bring out the implementation, by the narrator, of a real process of apprenticeship in symbolization. Thanks to the network of metaphors provided, the reader of John gradually learns to decipher the symbols.

Take light. The prologue of the Gospel (reading pact: > 9.2) has said that the Word was the true light coming to lighten the world (1.9). On hearing Jesus proclaim himself the 'light of the world' (8.12) the reader will understand the symbolic dimension of the healing of the man born blind (to see truly is to believe in Christ). He will also understand why Judas leaves Jesus by night (13.30), why Mary of Magdala goes to the tomb while it is still dark (20.1), and why the disciples of Chapter 21 have fished all night without catching anything, until they meet the risen Christ in the morning. The metaphor 'light of the world' functions as a signal given at the beginning of the book which makes the reader sen-

sitive to the symbolism of light/darkness each time it appears subsequently.

There is the same scenario with water. The symbol appears in John 2 (Cana), then in John 3 (Nicodemus), in John 4 (the Samaritan woman), in John 5 (the paralysed man of Bethesda), etc. up to the crucifixion, where it flows from the side of Christ (19.34), ironically released by the spear-thrust of a soldier. This enrichment of reading by the symbolic dimension explains why the Gospel must be constantly taken up again, reread, meditated on once more, so that the readers discover new symbolic potential in the text which will take them further into the fullness of meaning.

The establishment of a network of metaphors thus inserts readers into a process of initiation which leads them, step by step, towards a deeper understanding of the identity of the one towards whom the system of symbols points, the Christ of the Gospel. The readers constructed by this narrative strategy progressively enter into a language of the initiate, to which the text gives them access.

Check your knowledge

- Discover how, in the narrative of the ascension of Elijah (II Kings 2.1–18), the narrator plays on the symbolism.

METAPHORS OF LIGHT

An application: Mark or the destabilization of the reader

The rhetorical narrative of the Gospel of Mark aims at an effect which can be expressed in a formula: the deconstruction of the status of the initiate. Clearly different from Matthew, the narrator of the Second Gospel is a past master in thwarting 'predictable scenarios' in his readers.

Let's follow the collective character of the disciples. The call of the four fishermen (1.16–20) and Levi (2.14) and then their companionship with Jesus encourages a positive identification of the reader with the group. In 4.10–12 Jesus distinguishes them from 'those outside' who do not understand, by saying to them, 'To you is given the mystery of the kingdom of God'. So a line is drawn between the group of disciples, who benefit from the teaching of Jesus, and the crowds, for whom the teaching remains obscure. From now on everything seems clear . . . but the Marcan narration takes the opposite course to the expected scenario.

For immediately afterwards, in 4.13, the reader is surprised to read: 'And he said to them: "Do you not understand this parable? Then how will you understand all the parables?"' Here there is a complete reversal. The narratee, first of all excluded by a veil of opacity in 4.11, suddenly grasps that the disciples do not understand, so that he himself is now one of the insiders (see 112f. above). As for the insiders in v.11, they have become equal in v. 13 to 'those outside'. The veil of opacity has now excluded new victims. But if the narrative gives the readers an advantage over the disciple-initiates, the narrative mechanism of veiling is going to be reproduced in their case, as we shall see.

Meanwhile let's follow the disciples. Immediately after the discourse in parables, the story of the storm dramatizes the failure of their trust (4.35–41). When they return from their mission they fail to feed the hungry crowd (6.37); then the crossing of the sea makes them take the Lord to be a ghost (6.45–51). Both times the incomprehension in which the miracle of the loaves has left them is exposed (6.52; 8.14–21); the second time, their failure to understand is classed with that of the Pharisees in words from Isaiah, who asserted the hardening of 'those outside' (8.18). The moment that Jesus reveals his forthcoming passion openly (8.31), Peter by his refusal shows that he is not inside but outside. As for the transfiguration, taken as an epiphany of the Son but hiding the cross, this ends up with an order for silence which is observed without understanding (9.10). The flight of the disciples far from the cross and their absence from the empty tomb will do the rest.

We see that the narrative systematically deconstructs the status of initiates established in chapter 4

of the Gospel. Transforming the group of initiates and non-initiates, the insiders and outsiders, it destroys the notion of privilege linked with confidential information. The Gospel of Mark does not protect a secret; it narrativizes its dissolution.

The avalanche of unanswered questions

The number of questions which figure in the Second Gospel is really amazing. R.M.Fowler mentions 114 of them, 77 of which go unanswered (*Let the Reader Understand*, 132 n.8). The majority of these remain without a direct answer at the level of the story, but implicitly call for a response from the reader on the axis of communication. They are a bit like the nervous system of the narrative. Deriving from the characters, they enter into the narrative strategy without the readers at first perceiving questions that the narrator is addressing to them.

The narrative technique of the Gospel of Mark shines through clearly when we put the passage about the leaven of the Pharisees in parallel with the same passage as it has been rewritten by Matthew on the basis of the Markan narrative.

In Mark, because the disciples once again show their total incomprehension, Jesus reprimands them bitterly in the form of a tremendous series of unanswered questions (eight, two of which are followed by a single-word response). Matthew tones down the scene by keeping only five questions and ending the episode on a mitigating note: 'Then they understood. . .' The climate is at the opposite pole. As often in Matthew, the disciples assent to the teaching and understand the meaning of the words of Jesus, while in Mark they have no reaction and seem imprisoned in incomprehension.

In the Second Gospel, this narrative is followed by the healing of a man born blind. The reader cannot help seeing a double movement at work: those outside are healed, while those inside have a closed mind. At the level of the narrative, the readers certainly do not understand all that the disciples have difficulty in grasping. At least they become aware that the disciples are proving unintelligent. By

Mark 8.14–21	Matthew 16.5–12
The disciples had forgotten to bring bread and they had only one loaf with them in the boat. Jesus cautioned them, saying: 'Beware of the leaven of the Pharisees and the leaven of Herod.' They discussed among themselves the fact that they had no bread. Jesus was aware of this and said:	*When the disciples reached the other side they had forgotten to take bread. Jesus said to them, 'Beware of the leaven of the Pharisees and the Sadducees!' And they discussed it among themselves: 'We brought no bread.' But Jesus perceived this and said to them:*

Five questions
- *'Why are you discussing the fact that you have no bread?*
- *Do you not yet perceive or understand?*
- *Are your hearts hardened?*
- *You have eyes, do you not see?*
- *You have ears, do you not hear?*

Two appeals to the memory
- *Do you not remember when I broke the five loaves for the five thousand men, how many baskets full of pieces did you take up?'*
- *They said to him, 'Twelve.'*
- *'And when I broke the seven loaves for the four thousand people, how many baskets full of pieces did you take up?'*
- *They said, 'Seven.'*

Abrupt question
- *And he said to them, 'Do you not yet understand?'*

Two questions
- *'O you of little faith, why do you reflect on the fact that you have no bread?*
- *Do you not yet understand?*

Two appeals to the memory
- *Do you not remember the five loaves for the five thousands, and how many baskets you gathered?*
- *Or the seven loaves for the four thousand and how many baskets you gathered?*

Question extended by an explanation
- *How do you not understand that I was not speaking to you about bread when I said to you, "Beware of the leaven of the Pharisees and the Sadducees!"'*

Final relief
Then they understood that he had not told them to beware of the leaven in bread but of the teaching of the Pharisees and the Sadducees.

means of the series of unanswered questions the readers come to place themselves closer to Jesus than his friends seem to be. On the level of the story, the insiders become outsiders. On the level of the implicit commentary, the readers who were outsiders become insiders. This indicates that the insiders, benefiting from the start from a considerable privilege ('To you is given the mystery of the kingdom of God', 4.11), risk missing the meaning of the events; they are not at all assured of keeping their position; on the contrary, the threat of blinding falls constantly on them, above all when previously they thought that they had arrived at a correct view. On the other hand, to the degree that they remain open and receptive in their quest, the outsiders can in turn benefit from an enlightenment which introduces them into the mystery; however, once they draw any assurance from this they are pushed out again. There is no guarantee of remaining what one has become.

In quite an opposite way to this scenario, the readers of Matthew find themselves progressively structured by the unfolding in the Gospel of the 'mysteries of the kingdom of heaven', which is given them to know: these mysteries are expounded in the five great discourses of the Matthaean Christ (Matt.5–7; 10; 13; 18; 23–25). Mark's narrative in turn disorientates and reorientates the readers, teaching them the vulnerability of any knowledge by the narrative dramatization of the failure of the disciples.

However, theologically that is not the last word in the Gospel of Mark. For while planning the deconstruction of the status of the initiate, the narrative relates how the mystery unfolds despite everything: it sends the reader in search of examples to deliberately marginal figures: a Syro-Phoenician woman (7.24–30), a crowd hungry for the word (6.34; 8.2); a father who confesses unbelief in his belief (9.24). Under the cross it will be the turn of the Roman centurion to recognize the Son of God (15.39). Better still, it will be the disciples who have failed whom the Risen Christ will precede into Galilee. Through the scenario of failure runs the thread of grace. But where does this game of deconstructing models lead? What awareness does Mark want to arouse in the reader? What understanding of believing existence is induced in the reader by such a sequences of falls and new beginnings?

In response, it is necessary to remember that here the readers do not identify themselves with one figure in the narrative; the understanding results from an accumulation of knowledge disseminated through the narrative. In the event, the readers see the perplexity of the disciple-initiates throughout the narrative. But at the same time they watch the incomprehensible faithfulness of Jesus towards them: the last supper in Jerusalem is the culmination of this faithfulness (Mark 14.17–25). However, the readers do not stop at this crisis in knowledge, since unlike the disciples, they are not absent from the passion. They witness the spectacle from which the disciples have fled: the arrest of the master, his unjust trial, the outrages inflicted on him, his death. As Werner H.Kelber puts it: 'In thus observing not only what the disciples could observe but also what was outside their scope, the readers progressively assume the role reserved for the disciples. That makes the readers move. . . to the level of new initiates' (*Récit et révélation*, 408–9).

Do we have to conclude from this that the readers, who have a knowledge which is hierarchically superior to the disciples (> 5.8), are called to witness the débâcle of the disciple-initiates with the sole aim of seeing their own knowledge confirmed? Must we think that the readers of Mark are made to witness the failure of the disciples to be better established in a state of theological certainty? Not at all. For the narrative has not prepared the readers for what they are allowed to witness. It is one thing for Jesus to die a brutal death, delivered into the hands of the Romans, in conformity to what had been predicted (Mark 8.31); it is another thing for him to feel the absence of God in this death (Mark 15.34): the event exceeds the prediction. It had been foretold that after three days the Son of man would be snatched from death (Mark 8.31; 9.9), but not that the epiphany of the Son would be recognized by a Roman soldier at the very nadir of the absence of God (Mark 15.39). The resurrection had been announced, but not this news of a Nazarene who has already left for Galilee, driving the terrified women far from the tomb (Mark 16.8).

So we see that if the narrative gives the readers an advantage over the disciple-initiates, the narrative mechanism of veiling is reproduced for them. At the moment when, in the absence of the disciples, the narrative takes charge of the readers, it makes them experience the same interference in their knowledge. Thus every posture of theological knowledge is interrogated, questioned by the narrative. By virtue of the narrative, the readers have become privileged witnesses of the epiphany of the Son of God; but do they understand it? Will we have to repeat in connection with them: 'They did not understand this word and feared to ask him' (9.32)?

For further reading

J. N. Aletti, *Quand Luc raconte. Le récit comme théologie*, Lire la Bible 115, Paris: Éditions du Cerf 1998, 69–112 (syncrisis in the book of Acts).

U. Eco, *Lector in fabula*, Paris: Grasset 1985 (interpretative co-operation of the reader).

W. Iser, 'Interaction between Text and Reader', in S.R.Suleiman and I.Crossan (eds), *The Reader in the Text*, Princeton: Princeton University Press 1980, 106–19 (interaction between text and reader).

V. Jouve, *La Lecture*, Paris: Hachette 1993, 43–63 (the text as a programming of reading).

Jean Duvet (1485–1570), *The Angel gives St John a Book to eat* (engraving).
Louvre (Rothschild Fund).

10

The act of reading

The previous chapter has familiarized us with the idea that the text attains its fulfilment in reading (>9.1). Reading is the action by which the literary work is led to its destination, or rather to those for whom it is destined: the circle of readers. Narrative criticism concentrates all its attention on this movement by which the text, escaping its author and its original readership, finishes its course outside itself in the act of reading. Thus 'the text, the orphan of its father, the author, becomes the adopted child of the community of readers' (P.Ricoeur, *Eloge de la lecture*, 403).

But we must be careful: the encounter between the text and the reader is not a tranquil embrace. Between the solidity of the text and the apparent infinity of its readings there is a dialectic which makes reading the place of an irreducible tension.

On the side of the reader, reading is an experience in which the whole subjectivity of the person is invested. The experience can vary: we read for pleasure, we read to discover, our emotions are moved by reading and we learn from reading. There are no readers whose way through the text coincides exactly with that of their neighbours.

On the side of the writing, the text does not remain inert. When read, the text acts on the reader like a recumbent statue which reading arouses. To write a text in effect corresponds, on the part of an author, to discernible matters of performance: to distract, convince, move, inform. Besides, one effect can hide another: under the appearance of amusement (to tell a story is also to divert) the narrative quite often works to persuade readers to question

the values which organize their life. The opposite is particularly true of biblical narrative: in choosing to tell a story, the biblical authors deploy a narrative rhetoric which aims to convince without neglecting the pleasure of the narrative. The Latin poet Horace said: 'He wins all the votes who mixes the agreeable with the useful, and who both charms and instructs the reader' (*Ars poetica* 343).

How is the conflict between the effect sought by the text and the royal freedom of the reader played out? Can one explain the action of the text beyond itself? How, when occupied in deciphering the sense of the text, do readers expose themselves to the return effect of the text on them? To discover this, let's listen in to the act of reading. Paul Ricoeur provides the necessary instruments for thinking about the interplay between the text and the reader (10.1). The difference between effect and reception, sense and signification will then occupy us; this will be the occasion to raise the question of the limits of interpretation (10.2). The reflection will end on the ultimate aim of the reading (10.3).

10.1 The world of the narrative and the world of the reader

Why, Ricoeur asks himself, the success of the narrative? If telling a story is such a widespread act of communication, it is because the narrative makes it possible to configure time. Telling a story is a means of understanding available to human beings (oneself). Whereas Aristotle defines the narrative as the

MIMESIS I

MIMESIS II

MIMESIS III

Mimesis I	world to which the narrative refers	prefiguration
Mimesis II	world of the narrative	configuration
Mimesis III	world of the reader	refiguration

arrangement of facts within a plot, Ricoeur adds this other factor which constitutes narration: 'Time becomes human time to the extent that it is organized after the manner of a narrative way; narrative, in turn, is meaningful to the extent that it portrays the features of temporal experience' (*Time and Narrative* I, 3).

But if telling a story consists in constructing a plot in temporal existence, how does the relationship work out between what the narrative relates and what the reader experiences? To offer a theory of this relationship, Ricoeur borrows another notion from Aristotle: *mimesis*. To tell a story is to show *mimesis* (again according to Aristotle), i.e. to represent the action by discourse. *Mimesis* is this gesture of creative imitation and representation from which narrative discourse is born: by imitation and representation we are to understand the dynamic process by which the story-teller transposes and configures an experience of the world in his story. Thus a Gospel miracle narrative results from the activity of the storyteller, who selects facts, systematizes them and attributes them to causes (the healing follows a prayer, which itself is usually prompted by a request).

So we see that the narrative is at the intersection of two worlds: before the text, the world experienced by the author; after it the world in which the reader lives. To understand the act of reading calls for a reconstruction of the whole arch of operations by which a work, prompted by an experience, in turn has an effect on the reader. It is a matter of reconstructing 'the set of the operations by which a work lifts itself above the opaque depths of living, acting, and suffering, to be given by authors to

readers who receive it and thereby changes their acting' (*Time and Narrative* I, 53).

Ricoeur schematizes this course as three stages: *mimesis* I (before the narrative), *mimesis* II (narrative) and *mimesis* III (after the narrative). This trilogy takes up the classic stages of going through the text: production/text/interpretation, defining them in an original way.

The three *mimesis*

Mimesis I denotes the preunderstanding of the world and human action common to the author and the reader. This is the anchorage that the narrative composition finds in the practical comprehension of the reader: telling a story postulates that the author and reader share the same perception of human action and its symbolism (to know what it means to eat or to raise one's hand in a meeting). Basing itself on this common grammar, *mimesis* I is the prefiguration of the narrative world which the narrator will unfold; it will allow the reader to reconstruct the story through the narrativization (which is *mimesis* II).

Mimesis II is the stage of narrative configuration or emplotment. Strictly speaking it is the moment in the narrative when thought snatches itself from immediate experience and becomes text: from a chaos of events it draws a plot which takes temporality into account and puts in place a network of characters. 'This configurational act consists of "grasping together" the detailed actions or what I have called the story's incidents of the story. It draws from this manifold of events the unity of one temporal whole' (*Time and Narrative* I, 66).

After the narrative, **Mimesis** III corresponds to what is called application or appropriation: the readers appropriate to themselves the world of the event and import it into their own world. This is the moment when the readers note the impact of the world of the narrative (with its value system, its apparatus of convictions, its programme of life) on their own view of the world and decide whether or not to adopt this view of things. This stage is the stage of interpretation proper: 'What must be interpreted in a text is a proposed world that I could inhabit and wherein I could project one of my own-most possibilities' (*From Text to Action*, 86).

Here we find once again the mimetic character of narration. In so far as it represents human action, the narrative offers a model of human experience and puts forward a vision of reality to adopt: to apply this view of reality to the world of the reader is an operation which Ricoeur suggests should be called refiguration. 'To follow a story is to actualize it in reading it' (*Time and Narrative* I, 76). So we see that the moment of *mimesis* III by which readers appropriate to themselves the world of the work does not belong exclusively to the readers' psychology but still to the work itself.

In short, *mimesis* I is the stage of the prefiguration of the human world; mimesis II *results from the narrative construction* of an experience of the world, constructed with the aid of the plot; mimesis III organizes the refiguration of the readers' experience by appropriating the view of the story's world. The act of reading accompanies the configuration of the story and actualizes its capacity to be understood.

Necessary distance

One conclusion follows if we accept Ricoeur's paradigm of the three *mimesis*: for a reading to be authentically an experience, it is necessary that the text (*mimesis* II) does not correspond at every point with the world of the reader (*mimesis* III). If the world of the narrative and the world of the reader can be superimposed, the reading only produces a mirror effect. The readers rediscover themselves. On the other hand, the greater the distance between narrative and reader, the more the return to the world of the reader will raise fruitful questions. 'When he is confronted with difference and not with similarity, the subject has the possibility, thanks to the reading, of rediscovering himself,' remarks Vincent Jouve (*La lecture*, 97), who describes the reading as regressive or progressive depending on whether the text plays on similarity or difference.

Against any immediate appropriation of the text it is necessary, with Ricoeur, to emphasize the otherness as a fundamental dimension of the relationship to the text. In other words, the otherness of

---

READING: CONSTRAINT AND FREEDOM

'The paradox of reading is that on the one hand it is the prisoner of the text as it is, and to understand the text, it has to bow to it without obtaining more precise or supplementary information on the spot. But on the other hand it can enjoy considerable freedom within these limits: when although the text is fixed, the reader can operate between the elements which are made up of comparisons and relationships that the author had not necessarily foreseen. So the reader can benefit from this paradox to discern unexpected meanings in the text. In the current practice of reading, this interplay between constraint and freedom takes place without the reader always being aware of it and without it being done deliberately. Nevertheless, any interpretation of a text sets these two aspects of the process going: grasping the first (or 'literal', according to the current but ambiguous expression) sense of the text and discerning in it latent significations which can be the projection of the tastes and opinions of the reader' (M.P.Schmitt and A.Viala, *Savoir-lire*, 14).

the text is an indispensable condition of the experience of reading.

This remark is very important for reading the Bible. It makes us aware that the distance (historical, cultural) of the biblical texts, while a handicap for an immediate actualization, in reality functions as a condition of the possibility of an authentic quest for meaning. It is necessary to postulate a strangeness of the text in the reader's world, which makes reading an operation of decontextualization (the plot is torn from the historical world to which it relates) and recontextualization (in the current world of the reader).

10.2 Two aspects of the act of reading

Objections could be made to Ricoeur's reading, and the debate on the reader's freedom could be started again. Hasn't it missed out the capacity of readers to engage in or withdraw from the action of the text on them? This objection is correct: the reader is sovereign. Without that, it is impossible to understand the colourful history of readings of the biblical text. At this point in the reflection it is important to keep in mind the distinction between the *effect* of the text (determined by the work) and the *reception* of the text (which depends on the freedom of the receiver). This duality restores its paradoxical dimension to the act of reading: on the one hand every reading must bow to the text, down to its smallest details; on the other hand the receiver can 'play' with the elements of the text. But to what degree?

Let's refine things further. The act of reading comprises a perceptive aspect and a receptive aspect. To perceive the offer of a world made by the narrative corresponds to the first aspect: to receive it in order to guide one's own view of the world corresponds to the second. The effect of the text is a potential the power of which is actualized through its reception by the reader.

Things can be put in yet a different way, by adopting a polarity between the objective and the subjective. The subjective reception by the reader is conditioned by the objective effect of the text. It is because the book of Genesis tells me the story of the creation of the world (objective aspect) that I can adopt a position on the origin of life (subjective).

Sense and signification

Ricoeur, again, has suggested distinguishing between the two aspects of the act of reading by the duality between sense and signification. The sense is acquired from reading at the end of the stage of deciphering the work; it is located at the level of *mimesis* II. The signification is 'the moment of taking up the sense by the reader, his effectuation of it in existence' (*The Conflict of Interpretations*); this is *mimesis* III. Thus the act of reading mixes and links these two elements: on the one hand the grasp of the sense of the text, and on the other the reaction of readers to what they have perceived in the text. We will say that in the first case the text has been explained and in the second case it has been understood.

Grasping the sense is an analytical operation which requires the reader to be attentive to the signals for comprehension sent out by the text. This operation requires to be controlled: the mandate for verifying the grasp of sense falls to exegesis (whatever instruments for reading it uses: historical criticism, narrative criticism, rhetorical criticism, symbolism). At this stage the criteria of a good reading are objective; they verify the precision and relevance of the grasping of the text.

The moment the world of the text migrates in the direction of the world of the readers, another position is required of the readers: their appreciation of the value of the world which is offered them, in other words their judgment on the truth of the text. The signification that they accord to the work depends on this judgment, which will decide whether (or not) they recognize in it a truth to be integrated into their lives. The quest for signification is typical of a believing reading of the Scriptures.

Readers confronted with the Sermon on the

Mount will orientate their reading on the quest for sense: they will be interested in the structure of this sequence, in the injunctions made to the readers, in Jesus' position on the Law, the references to Jewish piety, etc. Their conclusions can be discussed, in some cases falsified, by another reading. On the level of signification, readers will ask whether they acknowledge the saying which says 'happy are the poor' and calls on them not to worry about the morrow, a truth which orientates their lives.

Not to be confused

So sense and signification are not to be confused. Normally the former precedes the latter, even if reading very often knows a coming and going: interest in the sense arouses curiosity about a possible signification, and the desire on the part of readers to integrate this into their lives relaunches the quest for sense. In any case, the desire to understand must of necessity accept that it has to go by way of explanation.

To sum up. For an act of reading to be realized, a chain of operations has to be performed, aimed at identifying the sense, and then building up the signification of the literary work. The quest for sense, determined by the indicators distributed through the text, notes the effect sought by the narrator: its result can be argued for or falsified on the basis of the text. On the other hand, building up the signification of the text calls for the subjectivity of the reader, to such a degree that in this respect results will vary considerably. The stability of meaning can be contrasted with the variability of the reception of the text, i.e. the fluctuation in the establishment of its signification.

Illegitimate readings?

Is every reading legitimate? Even if there is no true sense of a text, as Valéry remarked, can one say that interpretation can vary infinitely?

Umberto Eco has tackled this question in *The Limits of Interpretation*. According to him, the read-ing oscillates in an unstable equilibrium between the freedom of the interpreter and faithfulness to the text. The variability of the reading must not be deployed to the detriment of what he calls 'the rights of the text': these are the constraints on reading signified by the text, the restrictions it imposes on interpretation, which mean that one reading is desirable while another is not. Contrary to the deconstructionist current, Eco calls for respect for the resistance of the text to an uncontrolled deployment of readings.

It is enough to remember the procedure of explicit commentary (> 8.1) to confirm how well-founded this position is. When the narrator of John 12.6 comments, 'This he said, not that he cared for the poor but because he was a thief, and as he had the money box he used to take what was put into it' (this is in connection with Judas' protest at the anointing of Jesus), it is evident that he is dismissing one reading of Judas' discourse to favour another. There is an opposite example in John 13, where the same narrator makes two readings of the gesture of the foot-washing follow each other: one in connection with salvation (13.8: 'If I do not wash you, you can have no part with me'), the other of an ethical type (13.14: 'you too must wash one another's feet'). The same concern to guide the reader appears, in a restrictive way in John 12 and in a polysemic way in John 13.

The procedure is very skilful in the book of Jonah, where the narrator leaves the precise identity of the 'great fish' which swallows up the prophet very vague. Nevertheless he sprinkles enough signals through his narrative to channel the readers' imagination.

The approach of narrative criticism begins specifically in discovering the marks of the efforts made by the narrator to channel the interpretation. The quest for sense aims at coming as close as possible to the intention of the text (or, if you like, the intention of the implied author). So the legitimate interpretations are those that the text supports, which respect its constraints and take the maximum of its indications into account. But the plurality must be kept: the potential senses in the text are too unpredictable to dictate a single sense: the resistance of the text limits the plurality of meaning, without ever reducing it to one canonical meaning.

10.3 Reading in order to understand (oneself)

Reading is in constant oscillation between observation and implication. What is ultimately at issue in this coming and going between the text and the self and the self and the text?

'Ultimately, what I appropriate is a proposed world. The latter is not behind the text, as a hidden intention would be, but in front of it, as that which the work unfolds, discovers, reveals. Henceforth, to understand is to understand oneself in front of the text. It is not a question of imposing upon the text our finite capacity for understanding, but of exposing ourselves to the text and receiving from it an enlarged self, which would be the proposed existence corresponding in the most suitable way to the world proposed.' Once again we are following Paul Ricoeur (*From Text to Action*, 87–8) in this description of what is the issue in reading. This philosopher has developed the fine theme of narrative identity which readers have suggested to them in the act of reading when they explore the offer of a world made by the text.

Confronted with the text that addresses them, readers see possible selves deployed by the events of the narrative. Thus the texts confront them with a task which they have to undertake and in which no one will take their place. 'Yours is the duty to be done. Not a pupil in the neighbourhood' (Kafka).

To interpret is to play

The most striking paradigm of this self-questioning, by the text which models a possible reader, is in II Samuel 12. To King David, who in order to have Bathsheba for himself has sent Uriah to his death in combat, the prophet Nathan tells the story of the poor man; the rich man has taken his one lamb to offer to his guest. The king's indignation at this injustice calls for a brutal return from the world of the story to the world of the reader, 'You are the man.'

The parable of Nathan and its effect on David are a good metaphor for reading. Far from using discourse which would lecture David on his crime, Nathan uses the indirect communication of the story to provide the king with the model of a type of morality: usurping the rights of the weak. Judging this crime with indignation, David sees himself referred to his own world, to note that the plot of the story unfortunately corresponds to the plot in his life. The detour which the story allows offers the narrator the resources of fiction, and it is to the imagination of the readers that the story speaks while offering them their own possibilities.

THE WORLD OF THE NARRATIVE (MIMESIS II)

THE EFFECT OF THE NARRATIVE ON THE READERS WORLD (MIMESIS III)

That is why 'interpreting' is not just 'understanding' in the sense of a methodical intellectual investigation, but also 'playing', the word that we use for the musician interpreting a score or an actor interpreting a role. If for the readers, to interpret means refiguring their world from the world of the text, we can understand the sense of the word 'play' here: the narration offers them the opportunity to play out the plot of the text in the framework of their own existence, as a musician plays a score. In this encounter between the plot of the narrative and the plot of their lives, the text offers the readers a possibility of changing their personal plot: in a word, it offers them the possibility of becoming someone else. The gospel has a word to describe this movement: conversion.

The Bible tells itself

If the biblical authors have in the first place chosen to tell about God, rather than to offer discourses about him, it is basically because God makes himself known in history. But if, in order to tell the history which has been made between God and his people, the biblical authors have told stories, that is because of the powers of the narrative.

What are these powers?

- By its plot, the narrative brings sense and order into the disorder of the real. The legibility of the plot implies a legibility of the world. The biblical narrative postulates that life has a meaning, and affirms that the management of this meaning is to be sought in God.
- The narrative does not discourse on the essence of God. It does not expound a God who could be defined, contained in a name, in a concept. The God of the narrative comes in history and by history. He is historical, and so stories can be told of him. To read is to be led to say God by telling stories about him, by making history in one's turn.
- The passage from the world of the narrative to the world of the reader is a work of interpretation. In its ultimate stage, reading leads readers to face a world to be made, plots to be constructed around them, people to discover, the stamp of God to be perceived. Reading, with the reader hand to hand with the text, becomes the place where a Word arises from the text.

As J.-P. Duplantier says: 'Reading is like fishing with a line. The fisherman with a line sits on the bank of the river or lake: he knows how to watch the float which has been cast and the ripples of the pool, he knows how to interpret the moving vegetation and the colour of the water, but above all he believes that there are fish down there, and patiently casts his line and can wait . . . We are at the edge of texts to decipher the profusion of figures, to follow the outlines of meaning, to recognize the discourse which passes by, for we know that the Word is in there and that if it does not live there, at least it is there often' (*Sémiotique et Bible* 87, 1997, 55).

For further reading

U.Eco, *The Limits of Interpretation*, Bloomington: Indiana University Press ²1994 (legitimate and illegitimate readings).

P.Ricoeur, *Time and Narrative*, Vol.1, Chicago: University of Chicago Press 1990, 52–87 (the threefold mimesis).

- , *From Text to Action. Essays in Hermeneutics*, II, London: Athlone Press 1991, 75–88 (the distance necessary for interpretation).

- , *Oneself as Another*, Chicago: Chicago University Press 1992 (narrative identity).

11

How do we question the text?

This chapter suggests a battery of questions to orientate the reader in narrative criticism of the biblical narratives. The reading grid can be applied to any narrative, whether this is a brief episode or a sequence covering several chapters. It consists of a series of major questions, commented on (in italics) by sub-questions which make them more specific.

We suggest that readers begin by applying the eight series of questions in order; progressively, with the help of experience and growing narratological competence, they will be able to free themselves from this mould to form their own questions. The value of this grid is its exhaustiveness: it systematically interrogates the text from the point of view of its pragmatic effect, reviewing the whole of the questioning opened up by narratology. We shall not become involved in it without having three images in mind: a bunch of keys, a model which fails, and a crossroads.

A bunch of keys. The questions which follow are like a bunch of keys: the reader has all of them, but not all are useful for every text. Not all of them will open the locks of the meaning in every text. Each time it is important to find a good selection of keys for the text that one is in process of reading. Choosing good keys (those which open up an unexpected meaning) calls for know-how and intuition: thus with the aid of apprenticeship you will come to feel that one particular text is interesting from the point of view of its plot, while another arouses curiosity by the construction of its characters. The main thing is to mistrust the autoroutes of meaning.

To allow oneself to be re-routed from one's habitual reading by a questioning about the construction of a narrative is to offer a text to speak differently.

The model which fails. The models proposed by narrative criticism (quinary structure, the actantial scheme) do not dictate a stereotype to which every narrative must necessarily conform. They are like the cabinet-maker's rule, which does not serve solely to make furniture of the same dimension. The absence of transforming action in a plot or the impossibility of applying a neat closure to a narrative are precisely what make up the originality of the text. In other words, the difficulty of identifying an element of a structural model in a text does not perhaps lie in the defectiveness of the model or the incompetence of the reader but in the narrative itself, which reveals itself at this point and in so doing displays a specific profile.

The crossroads. Narrative criticism stands at a crossroads of other methods of reading the text: historical criticism, semiotics, rhetorical criticism, feminist criticism, etc. The results of these different readings can be linked to those of narrative criticism provided that the basic principle of narrative criticism, the axis of communication, is maintained. For example, if we find a concentric structure or a chiasmus in a text (rhetorical criticism), we will ask what effect of meaning is sought by it from the reader. If we integrate into the reading historical information about the monarchy in Israel, we will be careful not to confuse it with the way in which the text constructs the image of the king for the reader.

1. First approach

Observe how the narrative is constructed. How does the narrator set out to tell his story?
Examine the formal level: composition, style, language, type of narration. What is the effect of his way of telling the story?

Remember the cardinal principal of narrative criticism: linearity. The elements are considered according to the order in which they appear in the narrative.

Does the narrative contain one or more secondary narrators who tell a story in their turn? If so, look for the effects of this narrative technique.
Is the narrator present in the story that he is telling?

2. Closure of the text

Where does the story begin? Where does it end?
Suggest a closure and specify which criteria determine your choice (time, place, characters, theme, model or literary genre). The narratives often inherit a traditional cut: is it necessary to question this cut?

Divide the narrative into scenes.
How are the scenes linked together? What is the narrative progression?

Once the closure is fixed, what narrative indications refer backwards and forwards?
How has the narrative been prepared for beforehand? What situation does the narrative inherit from the point of view of the story? How does it go on afterwards?

Is the narrative part of a narrative sequence?
Is the sequence dominated by a hero or by a theme?

How is it constructed? What connections link the micro-narratives of the sequence?

3. The plot

What guideline assures the coherence of the narrative scenario?
Cut up the story in accordance with the quinary structure (1. initial situation; 2. complication; 3. transforming action; 4. denouement; 5. final situation).
Identify what constitutes the crux of the action (complication). Does the transforming action coincide with the turning point of the narrative? If there is a time lag, what is the effect produced? Can you see a relationship between stages 1 and 5, 2 and 4?

Is it possible to note the presence of modes of action (ought to do, want to do, know how to do, be able to do)?
Observe the possible pressure from an ought to do or a want to do. How do they influence the subject of the transforming action?

Who knows how to do and is able to do? How does the subject acquire these qualities? Did he possess them at the beginning?

Is there a combination of plots?
Combination works by linking, overlapping, inclusion or interlacing. What relationships are woven between episodic plot (micro-narrative) and unifying plot (macro-narrative)?

Is the plot one of resolution or revelation?
Distinguish between micro-narrative and macro-narrative.

4. The characters

Make a list of the characters (individual and collective) in the narrative.

What hierarchy does the narrative establish between the characters? Who are the protagonists? Who plays the role of the walk-on or the simple agent?

Differentiate between the round characters (several traits) and the flat characters (reduced to a single trait).

How do the characters serve the plot?
Use the actantial scheme: Despatcher/Receiver; Subject/Object; Opposer/Helper.

Does this scheme appear clearly or is it hidden from the eyes of the reader?

What characters lead the action? Who is going towards whom?

How does the narrator construct the characters?
What does the narrative say about the character (telling: denomination, information given on status or life-style)? What does it show (the action of the character)?

Follow the transformations of the characters: how their identities and relationships are constructed and are modified through the narrative. Who or what provokes these transformations? How and why? What is the relationship of the character with his or her past?

What feelings (empathy, sympathy, antipathy) does the narrative arouse towards the characters?

Observe the interplay of focalizations through the text.
Does the narrative give access to the inner feelings of a character (internal focalization)? Does it show what is taking place in such a way that the reader could observe it (external focalization)? Does it allow access to supplementary information which dominates time and space (zero focalization)?

From the point of view of knowing, is the reader's position superior, equal or inferior to that of the characters?

5. The setting

Observe the temporal indications. Does the chronology have a purely factual or a symbolic value?
Do the indications of time say anything about the type of time within which an action takes place (the night, the winter)? Does the narrative embody a view of 'monumental time' (which encompasses the origins and the end of time)?

What are the movements in space, the convergence and distancing of the characters?
Are the geographical facts set in a political scheme (Judaea/Galilee), a topographical scheme (sea/land; town/country), an architectural scheme (interior/exterior)? Which plane dominates: vertical, horizontal, circular?

What does the narrative teach the reader about the social setting of the story?
How are we to appreciate the role of these mentions in the narrative action?

6. Temporality

What variations are there in the pace of the story? Look for the pauses, the scenes, the summaries, the ellipses. Is there an alternation in the pace of the narrative?
What keys for reading do the moments of pause provide? What are the periods that the narrative passes over in silence? What does the narrator aim at in inserting summaries?

What sense does the rhythm of the narrative indicate?

Compare the order of the narrative with the order of events in the story as it can be reconstituted. Look for analepses and prolepses: what is their force, their breadth?
What is the sense of the biblical analepses (continuity, break, coherence between past and present)? Are they made by the characters or by the narrator? Do the prolepses issue in a conception of the end of time?

What sense is suggested by the order of the narrative?

Is the narrative singulative, iterative or repetitive?
What does the narrative condensation of the iterative narrative tell the reader? In the case of repetitive segments, carefully compare the different versions of the event. What tendency is at work in the narration

(simplification, focalization on a particular element, etc.)?

When a theme is taken up again (in one form or another), what effect of coupling is thus produced?

7. The narrative 'voice'

Who is speaking? How do we see the setting to which the narrator refers, his ideology, his hierarchy of values, his view of the world?

If the narrator makes massive intrusions into the story, what is he seeking to communicate to the reader by this procedure of apostrophizing the reader, of information and reflection on the reception of a saying?

Look for the narrator's explicit comments.

What is the significance of these explanatory glosses? Is the narrator resorting to scriptural arguments? Does he provide many explanations? Is he translating obscure terms for the reader? Is he pronouncing judgments on particular characters or actions?

Is he making his comments directly or through a character?

What does the narrator communicate to the reader indirectly or obliquely? Identify the implicit commentaries by the narrator.

Is the narrator making a play on intertextuality? Does he surprise the reader by paradoxes? Does he give an interpretative key by means of a mirror text? Does he provoke the reader's participation by describing a misunderstanding? Does he seek to win the reader through irony or humour? Does he employ the evocative power of the symbolic register? Does he leave part of the narrative in the shade, resorting to polyvalence or opacity (the gaps in the text)?

8. The text and its reader

In what way does the text programme the readers? What markers does it offer the readers on their way?

Look for the repetitive formulae, the connections. Does the narrative put the activity of several characters in parallel (syncrisis)? If so, with what intention?

How does the narrator play on the reader's capacity for prediction?

Does the text confirm or thwart the expectations of the reader? What does it seek to construct (or to deconstruct) in the reader's position?

What does the text choose not to say? What does it leave to the reader to complete concerning the probability, the logic of the actions, the symbolic language, the general signification (the sense of the episode in the main plot)?

What does the narrative not explain? What interpretative work does it invite the reader to do?

Can we find in the macro-narrative a reading pact sealed between narrator and narratee?

How does the peritext (preface, prologue, introductory phrase) orientate the reading?

For what implied reader is the narrative intended?
Identify the competences presupposed, the relationship with the event narrated, the possible complicity between implied author and reader.

Check your knowledge: the answers

Chapter 1, 1.4 p.17

What image of the implied reader arises from Judg.1.1–21 in terms of his knowledge, his culture and his experience?

When we read the beginning of the book of Judges, the major features of the profile of the implied reader can easily be found. The text constructs a reader who knows Joshua and the God of Israel. He also knows the situation of the Hebrew people in its conquest of the enemy, the Canaanites. The implied reader accepts that God can be consulted (he should know how, in principle in a sanctuary), that he speaks and thus intervenes in this war by designating the tribe of Judah (v.2). The reader knows the rules of war: the fate of the defeated (the thumbs and feet of Adoni-bezek are cut so that he can no longer draw the bow, vv.6–7; the practice of the ban on conquered cities, in which everything is destroyed, v.17); he also knows the customs of patriarchal culture: Caleb gives his daughter Achsah as wife to the conqueror of a city; however, Achsah takes the initiative in asking for springs of water from her father. The narrator – contrary to the rest of the book of Judges and to the historical facts – thinks that the reader is going to accept from the start the predominant role of the tribe of Judah in the conquest of the country, including Jerusalem. At least two reconstructions of the implied reader's theology and value-system can be proposed. The

first hypothesis is that the implied reader re-reads history through the prism of the literary genre, a historical narrative with epic features. The second hypothesis is that the narrative is addressed to a reader who is living in the exile or after the exile at a time when he has already lost the land which was promised and conquered. In this case his interpretation is directed towards an understanding of the dangers of imperialism and the colonialism from which they come. The reader is led to reconsider the place of God and that of the people in history.

Chapter 1, 1.4 p.17

How does one describe the relationship between narrator and narratee in Rev. 1.4–9?

First, it must be noted that the narrative authorities are clearly defined. The narrator is called John and he is addressing, from God, the seven churches which are in Asia. So he occupies the position of an apostle to well-defined Christian communities, while going beyond this limited setting (since the figure seven symbolizes fullness, John is transmitting a message which applies to the whole church). Secondly, the narrator and narratees are closely linked, on the one hand through the saving work of Christ (the threefold occurrence of the pronoun 'we' in vv.5b, 6a) and on the other hand in the sharing of the different aspects of the Christian condition

('Your brother, who shares with you in Jesus the tribulation and the kingdom and the patient endurance', v.9). Here the relationship between narrator and narratee is of an associative kind.

Chapter 2, 2.1–5 p.22

Compare the discourses of the episode 'Jesus enters Jerusalem' in Mark 11.1–10 and John 12.12–19.

Mark's narrative follows the events close to. The chronological order is respected: the procession approaches Jerusalem, Jesus sends two disciples, who find the foal and return with it, the crowd spreads out garments and branches, then acclaims 'he who comes'. Mark emphasizes above all Jesus' prediction about the foal (vv.1b-3) and its realization (vv.4–7a); this whole episode takes up 6 verses out of 10! The end of the narrative is barely sketched out (entering and leaving the temple). John proceeds in quite a different way. There is a strong emphasis on the acclamation of the crowd with the specific phrase 'the king of Israel' (cf. the importance of this theme in the Fourth Gospel: 18.33–37). John sums up (no trace of prediction); he interprets the entry into Jerusalem in the light of the fulfilment of scripture (v.16). At the level of the plot, this episode follows the 'sign' of Lazarus (vv.17–18) and stirs up the opposition of the Pharisees (v.19).

Chapter 2, 2.1–5 p.22

Compare the discourse of the Decalogue according to Ex.19.10–25; 20.8–21 with that according to Deut 5.1–5, 22.

In Exodus, an important place is left for the description of the *setting* of the proclamation of the Decalogue. The narrative dwells for a long time (16 verses of introduction and 4 of conclusion) on the formidable character of the theophany: voice, lightning, thunder, cloud, smoke and fire and a trembling of the whole mountain: the people quake with

fear and keep their distance. Deuteronomy too evokes the theophany, but in an indirect way: it is Moses who, much later, recalls these facts in the presence of all Israel. This is a narrative in the narrative; its function is to appeal to the collective memory of the past with the aim of addressing the readers in their own present, which is a time of crisis. Exodus depicts the event in a living way where Deuteronomy reports the facts at a distance; however, the form chosen allows the redactor to be incisive on another level: 'YOU were afraid. . . YOU did not go up the mountain' (Deut.5.5).

Chapter 2, 2.6 p.27

What is the status of the narrator Nathan in II Sam.12.1–15? What is the status of the narrator Peter in Acts 10.34–43? What is the status of the narrator John in Revelation 1.9–20?

In II Samuel 12.1–15, Nathan is a second (intradiegetic) narrator and he is telling the king a story from which he is absent (heterodiegetic).

In Acts 10.34–43 Peter too is an intradiegetic narrator (he is delivering a discourse within the 'main discourse' written by Luke, the author of the Acts of the Apostles). However, unlike Nathan he is present in the story that he tells in the house of Cornelius; his role as 'witness' (vv.39,41,42) puts him on a homodiegetic level.

In Revelation 1.9–20 John occupies the position of the primary narrator (he is the author of the book) and is thus on the extradiegetic level. As he intervenes in the story ('I was on the isle of Patmos'), one would call him homodiegetic.

Chapter 3, 3.3 p.34

Does the narrative of Saul's conversion in Acts 9 end in 9.19a, 9.25 or 9.30? What criteria can be used for making the closure?

The beginning of the narrative is marked on three levels: a clear designation of the protagonist (Saul), of the theme (persecution of the disciples of the Lord) and the places (Damascus/Jerusalem). On the other hand, there is no temporal precision. From 9.19b on, the action all takes place in Damascus and sets Saul and those who contradict him at odds: they want to kill him (a return of violence). There is no reason to support a closure in 9.19a (except the assimilation of the conversion of Saul to a healing narrative). From 9.26 the narrative concentrates on Saul's return to Jerusalem, his starting point (the same character and the same place); the theme of violence is initially toned down (fear of the disciples, then the welcome of Saul) before springing up again later (v.29, the Hellenists seek to kill him). For the persecution of him to stop the brothers have to send him to Tarsus. There then follows a summary: 'So the church. . . lived in peace' (v.31). Saul will not be mentioned again until 11.25. The indications converge in favour of a closure in 9.30.

Chapter 3, 3.3 p.34

Suggest a closure for the famous story of Cain and Abel (Gen.4).

Traditionally, the closure of the narrative is put at v.16. Cain, wandering but protected by a sign from the Lord, dwells in the land of Nod, an unknown country the name of which signifies 'wandering'. However, in narrative terms the section begins with the words, 'The man knew Eve, his wife; she conceived and bore Cain. . .' (v.1), and ends with the same mention in v.25 (Eve bears Seth, for God has granted another descendant in place of Abel). The addition of vv.17–24 gives quite a different aspect to the key character in the passage: Cain is described as a man who succeeds (he builds cities, and is the father of descendants who are creative in breeding, music and craftsmanship). Agriculture, art and technology are accompanied by the warlike activities of Lamech – a verbal violence aimed at keeping enemies at a distance (cf. the Marseillaise). Read in this way, the narrative leads us to discover behind the wonder that the development of civilization can

provoke that it is built upon the corpse of his brother by a man in search of roots, and that it is under constant threat of the escalation of violence.

Chapter 3, 3.5 p.39

Divide into scenes the appearance to Abraham by the oaks of Mamre (Gen.18.1–15). A promise is made to the patriarch here. Where do we find its fulfilment?

The text can quite easily be cut up into scenes:
First scene: the narrative indicates what is going to happen, the appearance of the Lord to Abraham (v.1).
Second scene: the narrative adopts the point of view of Abraham, who sees the three men, runs to meet them and asks them to stop (vv.2–5).
Third scene: Abraham has the meal prepared and serves it (vv.6–8).
Fourth scene: the announcement of the birth by the guests (vv.9–10).
Fifth scene: the story adopts the point of view of Sarah, who stays in the background and laughs (vv.11–12).
Sixth scene: the Lord (*sic!*) reaffirms his promise: a son will be born.
Seventh scene: Sarah denies that she laughed.

As we can see, this account of a promise calls for a fulfilment: that will not take place until 21.1–7. This narrative echoes the two themes evoked in Gen.18: the birth of a son and Sarah's laugh. In narrative terms, three episodes take place after the promise: Abraham's bargaining over Sodom, the destruction of the city and the second narrative in which Abraham passes off Sarah as his sister. The distance between the narrative of the promise (Gen.18) and that of its realization (Gen.21.1–7) allows the reader to mark the time of waiting and helps him to share the joy of Sarah, delivered from her shame. This delay in the realization will give all the more dramatic weight to Abraham's obedience in receiving the order to sacrifice his son.

Chapter 3, 3.5 p.39

Identify the links in the sequence of Gen.18–25 (character: Abraham).

The first part of the narrative presents the figure of Abraham as that of a nomad chief of great stature. He offers hospitality in an attentive and generous way. This feature will be reinforced by what Abraham undertakes for his clan: negotiating with the Lord in favour of Lot (Gen.18.16–33); protecting his wife, Sarah, by a subterfuge (Gen.20.1–18); organizing her burial (23.1–20). The place – the oak of Mamre – is equally loaded with history. Chosen by Abraham, it becomes the place of the promise and the announcement of the end of Sodom (Gen.18.1f.), and then that of the death of the patriarch. The whole sequence is marked by the advancing age of Abraham and Sarah and finally by their death. But thanks to the intervention of God represented by his angels, both die leaving behind direct descendants.

Chapter 3, 3.5 p.39

Note the 'sandwich' construction of Mark 3.20–35.

Mark 3.20–21: the crowd gathers and the kinsfolk of Jesus seek to intervene.

Mark 3.22–30: Jesus replies to the accusation of the scribes who have come from Jerusalem (in connection with the 'demonic' origin of his power);

Mark 3.31–35: Jesus' mother and brothers have him called; he replies to them with teaching on his true kinship.

There is a close relationship between the question of *kinship* and that of *origin*: in both cases the issue is the authority of Jesus. His family say, 'He has lost his head' (v.21). The scribes go beyond this: 'He has Beelzebul in him' (v.22); 'he has an unclean spirit' (v.30). Jesus replies to all these accusations by putting the original problem in a new, correct, setting: the witness of the Holy Spirit (v.29), which leads to doing the will of God (v.35). The two scenes (kinship/scribes) illuminate each other.

Chapter 4, 4.2 p.49

Establish the plot of the parable of the ten young women (Matt.25.1–13).

The initial situation is clearly described in v.1: ten young women take their lamps and go out to meet the bridegroom. The narrative tension arises from the fact that five of them are foolish and have not brought any oil (vv.2–3); in addition there is the delay of the bridegroom (v.5). The situation is thus constructed around a 'shortage': since they have no oil in reserve, their lamps go out (v.8). A first transforming action is aborted: the request addressed to their wise companions (vv.8–9). A second (the purchase of oil, v.10a) seems to succeed, but the final situation shows that it does not: the door is shut (v.10c) and the bridegroom refuses to be persuaded (v.12). The transforming action has not worked: this parable knows no denouement in the strict sense of the term... The shortage has certainly been made good, but too late! The time factor is crucial here: hence the exhortation to vigilance.

Chapter 4, 4.2 p.49

Establish the plot of the story of the demolition of the altar of Baal (Judg. 6.25–32).

Gideon is ordered by the Lord to demolish the altar of Baal, and then to build an altar to the Lord and offer him a bull as a holocaust (initial situation, vv.25–26). He caries out this order, but by night, for fear of the people of the city (virtual complication, v.27). He is not wrong: the inhabitants of the city call for the death of the guilty one (effective complication, vv.28–30). The intervention of Gideon's father constitutes the transforming action: 'If Baal is God, let him plead his cause himself, since Gideon has overthrown his altar' (v.31). The denouement takes place immediately: the people of the city accept this suggestion and give Gideon the name Jerubbaal ('Let Baal argue his cause against him', v.32). This suggests the final situation: Gideon will be able to take command of the people and conquer Amalek, the oppressor of Israel.

Chapter 4, 4.2 p.49

Where do you locate the dramatic tension and the pivot in the narrative of the healing of ten lepers (Luke 17.11–19)?

Since this is a healing narrative, the complication is created by the sickness, in this case leprosy. The pivot then appears in v.14b: 'Now while they were going there, they were cleansed.' This healing, noted without any emotional intensity, arouses hardly any reaction on the part of the reader. On the other hand, the tension increases a notch the moment one of the ten – the text says specifically that he is a Samaritan – returns to Jesus and throws himself at his feet, filled with gratitude. The tension continues to mount with Jesus' reaction: 'And where are the nine others?' (v.17). The reader understands that the essential point is going to come at this moment. In fact for this stranger the physical healing is combined with a liberation deep down: 'Your faith has saved you' (v.19). The words of Jesus bring the dramatic tension to its climax. It is then possible to re-read the story in quite a different way. . .

Chapter 4, 4.4 p.54

Linked plots: note the effect of linking in the sequences of the ten plagues of Egypt (Ex.7.8–11.10). How is Pharaoh's attitude presented to the reader?

There is a torrent of mentions of the hardening of Pharaoh's heart: 7.13, 22; 8.15; 9.12, 35; 10.1, 20, 27; 11.10. His refusals are noted in 8.11,28; 9.7. The opening formulae ('the heart of Pharaoh remained hardened'; 'Pharaoh refused') give way to an expression which marks more the definitive character of the attitude of the king of Egypt: 'The Lord hardened Pharaoh's heart' (from the sixth plague, in 9.12, and then for the eighth and ninth plagues). The narrative of the plague, before the departure from Egypt, itself ends with a conclusion in the form of a summary: 'Moses and Aaron did all these wonders before Pharaoh; but the Lord hardened Pharaoh's heart, and he did not let the people of Israel go out of his land' (11.10). The gradation is impressive. The reader grasps that the point of no return has largely been passed.

Chapter 4, 4.4 p.54

Overlapping: what particular position does the scene of the ascension occupy in Luke's work (Luke 24 and Acts 1)?

In the Third Gospel, the narrative of the ascension, given in two verses (24.50–51), represents the last passage in which Christ is the subject of the action ('he parted from them and was taken up to heaven'). After this scene, the evangelist concludes with the return of the disciples to Jerusalem and their joyful adoration in the temple. It is interesting to note that Luke again uses the motif of the ascension in his second work, the Acts of the Apostles, but this time as a starting point (1.6–11). This micro-narrative looks a bit like the chain which links the two parts of Luke's work. In any case it allows the two macro-narratives to be interlocked. So they are grafted together on the themes of presence and absence or, if you like, of communion and separation.

Chapter 4, 4.4 p.54

Inserted plots: the book of Revelation is constructed round great sequences called 'sevens': the seven letters to the churches (2–3), the seven seals (6.1–8.1), the seven trumpets (8.6–11.19), the seven cups (16). Note the alternation which arises, just before these sevens, between the 'heavenly' and 'earthly' scenes.

Each time, a seven is announced before it unfolds; between the announcement and the execution there is a scene relating what happens in the heavenly liturgy. This gives us interlaced sequences: heaven/earth/heaven/earth. . .

The construction of the whole is aimed at emphasizing the close relationship which exists between the two worlds: a heavenly event has immediate repercussions on earth. Furthermore, the sevens are interlocked: the seventh element is never described, but opens the next cycle (see the table below).

Chapter 4, 4.6 p.56

Is the plot of Exodus 17.1–17 (Massah and Meribah) a resolution or a revelation plot?

Apparently the narrative develops a resolution plot. The Lord, with Moses as his intermediary, gives water to the thirsty people. However, a closer reading brings out a revelation plot: the thirsty people murmur against Moses and against God; they question the liberation from Egypt when confronted with the risk of death (complication); God then intervenes (transforming action, vv.5–6a) through Moses (complication, v.6b); the final situation (v.7) seals the rebellious attitude of the people who have put God to the test with the name of a place, Massah and Meribah. Through this episode of the journey through the wilderness it is revealed who is the Lord, who is the people and who is Moses (a revelation plot rather than a simple resolution of a lack of water; besides, we are not told that the people drink it).

Chapter 4, 4.6 p.56

Establish the plot of Luke 10.29–37 (the Good Samaritan) and of 10.38–42 (Martha and Mary). How do these episodic plots fit into the unifying plot of Luke 10.25–42?

The sequence in 10.25–42 is opened with the lawyer's question about eternal life. Jesus replies with the Law (10.26–27), but the lawyer's question 'Who is my neighbour?' starts the questioning again. The plot of the parable of the Good Samaritan is constructed on the question about the neighbour: the Samaritan becomes the neighbour of

Announcement of the seven	Heavenly scene	Unfolding of the seven ('earthly' scene)
Order to write to the seven churches (1.11)	Vision of the Son of man (1.12–20)	Messages to the seven churches (chs.2–3)
Vision of the book sealed with seven seals (5,1)	Vision of the lamb once slain (5.2–14)	Opening of the seven seals (6.1–8.1)
Vision of the angels with seven trumpets (8.2)	Vision of the angel with the golden censer (8.3–5)	Sounding of the seven trumpets (8.6–11.19)
Vision of the angels with the seven plagues (15.1)	Vision of the crystal sea and the temple (15.2–8)	Overturning of the seven cups (ch.16).

the wounded man to the degree that he shows compassion towards him (see how the question in v.29 is turned back on the questioner in v.36). The plot of the episode of Martha and Mary is set in a debate which poses the alternative of diaconia or listening to the Word, but what is its theme? In fact, the unifying plot of Luke 10.25–42 develops from the lawyer's question (v.25), and the twofold commandment to love which he gives in response to the starting point in the Law (vv.26–28). In this context, the parable of the Good Samaritan reveals the force of love of neighbour; the episode of Martha and Mary clarifies the prior orientation of the one who loves God with all his heart. So the two micro-narratives are a commentary on the twofold commandment to love. Let us also note that after a reminder of the way in 10.29–35 (cf. 9.51 and the way to Jerusalem, where Jesus will face death), the episode of Martha and Mary offers a unique place for benefiting from the good part: to be 'seated at the feet of Jesus and to hear his word', i.e. to be a disciple.

Chapter 5, 5.2 p.62

What hierarchy of characters does the narrative of the confrontation between David and Nathan present (II Sam.12.1–25)?

In the first verse the narrative identifies the principal character for the reader: the Lord, who sends the prophet Nathan to King David. If Nathan acts in the name of God, with his authority, the narrative sees to it that the character David is left his place as king. The other characters (Bathsheba and the child) are lower in the hierarchy – walk-ons. The elders of the house of David (v.17), the servants (v.21) are agents. The confrontation between Nathan and David comes about by means of a parable. The narrative parable takes time to construct an affectionate relationship between the poor man and his lamb. The action of the rich man, who takes the lamb away from him to offer to a passing guest, appears all the more hateful. David's indignation is such that he pronounces a judgment against which

there us no appeal: 'As the Lord lives, the man who has done that deserves to die' (v.6). Nathan has only to deliver the final thrust by declaring, 'You are the man!' (v.7). Thus by means of the parable the narrative ensures that the two protagonists keep their roles: Nathan the prophet remains in his role of God's spokesman; David the king remains in his role as judge by pronouncing a judgment, in this case against himself.

Chapter 5, 5.2 p.62

How do you classify the characters (protagonists, walk-ons, agents) in the story in Luke 7.11–17, the resurrection of a young man at Nain?

Jesus appears from the start as protagonist, accompanied by walk-ons (disciples and a great crowd, v.11). Then the action moves towards another group, a funeral procession composed of a son, a widow and bearers (agents) and a considerable crowd (walk-ons). The narrative directs the reader's attention not to the dead son (who is defined in relation to his mother as an only child), but to the young man's mother. Seized with pity for her, Jesus restores the young man, raised, to his mother. So the woman is the protagonist before Jesus. The narrative makes the reader hesitate – as the titles of the pericope in our Bibles indicate – between the son and his mother. Is it not the place of the woman, and a widow at that, which is in question in Luke's community? The text works on this question narratively in the depths of the reader's mind. The fusion of the two crowds at the end of the narrative enlarges the backcloth of walk-ons. They give place to the word that is spread (a marker which refers back to the macro-narrative of Luke-Acts). And the readers progress in their recognition of the identity of Jesus, prophet of the liberating word.

Chapter 5, 5.3 p.64

Who are the actants in the story of the healing of Bartimaeus (Mark 10.46–52)?

As in all the healing narratives, we can presuppose from the beginning that Jesus occupies the role of Subject, and that the Object of his approach is the cure, envisaged as a sign of salvation. In this respect the Receiver is evidently Bartimaeus, while the Despatcher is not mentioned (it is God). The narrative specifies that the persistent faith of the blind man constitutes the Helper (v.48b, 52). The Opposer appears under the features of all those who rebuff Bartimaeus and tell him to keep quiet (v.48a). If we consider the text in isolation, and no longer in its context, we can also attribute to the blind man the role of Subject and Receiver (the Object still being the healing); at this moment Jesus is not a simple Helper but the Despatcher (the one who inspires Bartimaeus; cf. the title 'rabboni' and above all the sequel to the healing, v.25).

Chapter 5, 5.3 p.64

Construct the actantial scheme of the episode of the water of Massah and Meribah (Num.20.1–13).

At first sight it seems quite easy to identify the actants. The Despatcher is the Lord; the shortage (Object) is water (and therefore life); the Receivers are the Israelites; the operative Subject is Moses and Aaron; the Helpers are the word and the staff. The narrative ends with the punishment of the people of Israel for revolting against God (v.13). However, a second reading shows that the narrative is more subtle. The lack of water is linked to a challenge to Moses and Aaron from the people. There is no appeal against the sanction of the Lord, the Despatcher; they have not shown the holiness of God, they will not enter the promised land (v.12). So the scheme can be refined: the people (Helper) are the ones who reveal the lack and provoke Moses

and Aaron to action; the operative Subject is the Lord who, through the staff, acts and supports the people against Moses and Aaron; the latter obey the order with bad grace (Opposers) and as such are punished by the Lord. These two readings opt, one for a resolution plot (the lack of water), the other for a revelation plot (the Lord shows his holiness and takes up a position against Moses and Aaron's lack of faith). This twofold reading perhaps allows us to explain an enigma narratively: why does Moses strike the rock twice?

Chapter 5, 5.3 p.64

Construct the actantial scheme in the encounter between Philip and the Ethiopian eunuch (Acts 8.26–40).

The Subject appears clearly: it is Philip, sent by the 'angel of the Lord' (v.26), later called the 'Spirit' (vv.29, 39) – this is the Despatcher. The Receiver is none other than the Ethiopian eunuch. The Object is described as the 'good news of Jesus' (v.35) or, more simply, the 'good news' (cf. v.40). In fact this is knowledge of the divine plan, which issues in the baptism (vv.36–38). In this setting the reference to Scripture (here a passage of the prophet Isaiah and its fulfilment in the person of Jesus) plays the role of the Helper, while the absence of a guide (v.31) represents the Opposer – overcome by sending an interpreter in the person of Philip. The phrase 'What prevents me from receiving baptism?' attests the disappearance of all Opposers.

Chapter 5, 5.6 p.69

Observe how the narrator creates empathy for the Roman centurion in Luke 7.1–10.

The narrative takes time to describe the centurion. The narrator reconstructs his identity as a pagan and a soldier of the occupying forces: he is a man with an emotional attachment to one of his servants, who is at the point of death (v.2). A second feature is that it shows the respect of the centurion who, in Luke, does not meet Jesus himself. The request is transmitted by a delegation of Jewish notables. This distance is emphasized in what follows by the intervention of friends (another delegation), who report the words of the centurion and try not to make Jesus cross the boundary between the interior and the exterior of his people. For the centurion, the saying of Jesus – behind which stands out an authority higher than that of the emperor which legitimates his own authority – can cross this frontier effectively. The readers, who have felt sympathy for the centurion, are led to empathy through the admiration that Jesus has for him (v.9). Jesus' saying reverses the relationship between interiority and exteriority (those who find themselves inside – or believe that they are – and those who find themselves outside). The episode is a marker on the trajectory of Luke-Acts, relating the gathering of a new people including Jews and pagans.

Chapter 5, 5.6 p.69

What attitude does the narrator of the book of Job induce in the reader towards the hero of the book?

The first verse of chapter 1 locates the character straight away: a just man, with integrity, he fears God and keeps away from evil (the typical portrait of the faithful in Old Testament theology). The narrator does not content himself with an opening statement; he shows this man in action (1.4–5). The sympathy felt by the readers becomes even stronger the moment they become aware of the judgment uttered by the Lord: 'There is not his equal on earth' (1.8). The adversary then has a go at Job, which again furthers the sympathy towards him. This never becomes empathy in the first two chapters, since in them Job is depicted as a model without peer ('The Lord has given, the Lord has taken away, blessed be the name of the Lord' – 1.21, which finds an echo in 2.10). Empathy becomes possible from the dialogue in verse onwards (at 3.2), since then

the hero takes on a very human dimension, cursing the day of his birth – but this is almost another story which is beginning. . .

Chapter 5, 5.7 p.71

Observe how the story of David and Goliath (I Sam.17) plays on the telling and the showing of the characters.

The narrative takes time to describe the order of battle in the two camps (vv.1–3) and the champion of the Philistines, Goliath (vv.4–7; telling). His stature and the weight of his armour are beyond compare, as is the narrative of his incessant provocation of the Hebrew people. The challenge of the Philistine is described (vv.8–11, showing) or stated. Verse 16 (telling) is a reminder of the threat of the Philistine in the middle of the narrative of David's arrival (vv.12–22). David's intervention is described in the dramatic mode. He experiences opposition from his brothers. David also pleads his cause by a narrative: he has already fought against lions and bears (34–37). David confronts Goliath without any warlike equipment. David is said to be 'ruddy and comely in appearance' (I Sam.17.42, telling; cf. I Sam.16.12–13). This appearance provokes scorn on the part of the giant, who takes David for a child. The narrative allies the narrative mode and the dramatic mode to show how this frail boy without adequate weapons conquers the champion of the Philistines.

Chapter 5, 5.9 p.76

Identify the focalizations in the account that Jeremiah gives of his ministry (Jer.20.7–18). In what sense do they guide understanding of the passage?

In ancient literature and in the Bible it is rare for the reader to be able to get under the skin of characters. With some others (11.8–12.5; 15.10–21), this passage from Jeremiah is an exception. It introduces us to the prophet's inner debate with himself (internal focalization). The reader becomes the confidant of the prophet. Jeremiah appears human, frail and captivating. The elements of the narrative in external focalization allow the reader to follow what is happening for the prophet step by step (v.10). The reminder (in zero focalization) that the Lord defends the just and delivers the life of the poor from the evildoers (vv.11–13) only causes a supplementary shock. For with an abrupt denial the reader is again caught up into the prophet's inner turmoil as he curses the day of his birth (vv.14–18, where two internal focalizations frame v.15 in an external focalization).

Chapter 5, 5.9 p.76

Compare the narratives of Jesus' coming to Nazareth in Mark 6.1–6 and Matt.13.53–58 in terms of their focalizations. What is the special focalization of Mark's story?

The narratives of these two Synoptic Gospels are very similar from the point of view of focalizations. Both begin by telling their stories in external focalization: Jesus comes into his homeland and teaches in the synagogue. The reader is informed of the effect of his teaching on the hearers: they are struck (internal focalization). Their inner debate is detailed in direct discourse (external focalization). Then the reader again penetrates into the inner thoughts of the people of Nazareth: they are scandalized by him (internal focalization). Jesus castigates their refusal in a sentence: 'A prophet is only scorned in his own country. . .' (external focalization). The narrator goes on to indicate that Jesus cannot show his power of healing (zero focalization). Mark's narrative, unlike that of Matthew, sheds light on Jesus' attitude (internal focalization): he was amazed at their unbelief. Without piercing the mystery of the character of Jesus, the unveiling of his reaction – open amazement – provokes the readers and invites them to respond in faith in a responsible and autonomous way, to take the way of freedom (Mark

has been careful to indicate that this was the sabbath, the day of liberation).

Chapter 6, 6.2 p.80

Note the notations of time in Gen.50.1–14. What do they indicate about the process of mourning (mortal time) and the history of the people in Egypt (monumental time, cf. Gen.50.25; Ex.13.19)?

The burial of the patriarch Jacob, Joseph's father, gives rise to a cultural confrontation. The Egyptian rite is described in detail with an emphasis on the duration: forty days for the embalming (v.3), seventy days of mourning; when the impressive cortege arrives on the other side of the Jordan, Joseph celebrates seven days of mourning. The Canaanites – and the readers – have no difficulty in identifying with an Egyptian rite. However, this rite ends in the land of Canaan, the promised land. At the moment of his death Joseph asked the people of Israel to take his bones out of Egypt (Gen.50.25). Moses did not fail to do this (Ex.13.19). Thus the history of the deliverance of Israel also relates the final break with the land of slavery, to the point that no traces or memory of it remain.

Chapter 6, 6.3 p.82

Observe the oppositions in place and the movements in the narrative of the tower of Babel (Gen.11.1–11). What significance do they give to the episode?

The narrative plays with indications of place and space. The people who are united at the beginning are transformed into inhabitants dispersed 'over the whole surface of the earth'. The discovery of the plain is combined with an agreement on the plan: to build a city and a tower. A vertical is added to the horizontal of the plain, built by human hands. It goes with a concern to make a name for themselves. High though the tower is, the narrative shows the

Lord – not without irony – descending. Thus God 'forbids' the people's plan in a prophylactic way, confusing its one single language and then dispersing the people. The return to horizontality institutes and preserves the differences of languages and cultures.

Chapter 6, 6.3 p.82

John 18.28–19.16. Discover how the entrances and exits give rhythm to the trial of Jesus before Pilate. What sense is induced by this coming and going?

For a long time it has been known how the narrative of the trial of Jesus before Pilate is divided into internal and external scenes (external 18.29–32; internal 18.33–38; external 18.38–40; 19.1–3; external 19.4–8; internal 19.9–12a; external 19.12b-16). Over and above the cultic prohibition which prevents the Jews from entering the praetorium, this is a piece of staging. Pilate shuttles between the exterior – where the crowd cries out, urged on by the chief priests – and the interior, where he engages in dialogue with Jesus. Pilate is the governor. The movement of going out and coming in confirms that he is the one who rules. Isn't 'going out and coming in' a figure of style, a merismus, denoting the action of the governor (cf. I Sam.18.16; II Sam.5.2)? But Pilate is going to yield to the power of the crowd. Convinced of the innocence of Jesus, he progressively loses his authority and hands the prisoner over.

On the other hand, by his coherent attitude, Jesus, led into the praetorium and then to an indeterminate place for the parody of a coronation (19.1–3), and finally outside for the judgment (19.4–8), has a paradoxical authority. A travestied king, weak and ridiculed, he grows in the fulfilment of his mission, glorification and exaltation towards the Father.

Chapter 6, 6.4 p.84

What, broadly, is the social setting which can be seen behind the narrative of the arrest of Paul and then of his transfer to Caesarea (Acts 21.26–40; 22.22–23.35)?

A number of elements should be noted: 1. the split which exists between Jews and Romans (the occupying power); 2. the riot among the Jews when the profanation of the temple is threatened (21.27–31); 3. the existence of violent nationalist movements (21.13); 4. the irreconcilable opposition between Pharisees and Sadducees, even within the Sanhedrin (23.6–9); 5. the 'religious' character of the plot hatched against Paul (23.12); the concern of the Romans to keep order (21.31–32); 7. their sense of hierarchy (centurion – tribune – governor, 22.24–25 and 23.22–30); 8. the prestige attached to the title 'Roman citizen' (22.26–29; 23.27); 9. The scrupulous respect for Roman law (23.35). This simple list shows the narrator's esteem for the Roman world (Paul's life is saved three times by the intervention of the tribune: 21.32; 23.10, 23, 24).

Chapter 7, 7.1 p.89

What is the function of the summary in Matt.8.16–17, put in the middle of the scenes of Matthew 8?

After the Sermon on the Mount, Matthew brings together a series of miracle stories. Following the discourse, Jesus proclaims the good news in actions. He performs three healings: of the leper, the centurion's servant and Peter's mother-in-law. The summary allows the narrator to generalize Jesus' action: he frees from their ills the people who are brought to him, whether these ills alienate (possession) or affect the person from the outside (the sicknesses). The evangelist takes advantage of this to offer a theological perspective on the action of Jesus, quoting a text from Isaiah (53.4). For Matthew, Jesus is more than a miracle-worker; he fulfils the function of the Lord who has been announced. This passage illuminates the sequel to the story. While pursuing his actions of liberation, Jesus goes on to present himself in turn as the one who calls (8.18–22; 9.9) and the one who affirms his authority over the elements (8.23–27) and over the Law (9.10–17).

Chapter 7, 7.1 p.89

Find the pauses in the narrative of the making of the covenant on Sinai (Ex.24). What force do they give the narrative?

In the narrative of the making of the covenant, two pauses are arranged. The first (in v.10) prolongs the scene of the vision of God. This moment in the narrative is a culminating point: as the narrator and the reader must know, no human being can see God and remain alive (cf. Ex.33.20). The description dwells on this vision for a moment, even if it means using conventional images (cf. Ezek.1.26); then the narrative mentions – as an exceptional fact – that God does not lay hands on them. The second pause (in v.17) emphasizes the perception of the glory of God on the part of the people. It is a fire (sign of the theophany). This light, a manifestation of the divine presence, allows the people to participate in the event while remaining at the foot of the mountain.

Chapter 7, 7.1 p.89

After relating the birth of Moses, the book of Exodus does not speak of his adolescence (Ex.2, see v.11). How are we to interpret this ellipse?

The story of Moses begins with a birth narrative (Ex.2.10), which allows the reader to know his identity and to understand: (a) why Moses does not know about the situation of his oppressed people (v.11); (b) why the liberator of Israel will find it difficult to be accepted by his brothers (v.14). The narrator does not take the trouble to relate Moses' Egyptian education. In narrative terms, a parallel can be established between this ellipse and the

omission of the first part of the name 'Moses', which should bear the name of a divinity, e.g. Thutmoses, 'the god Thot is born'. Moses, by virtue of his name, is in search of God. The narrator deliberately chooses to speak of the mission of Moses with the God who will reveal his name to him (Ex.3.14). By that he shows his theological support for the God of Israel.

Chapter 7, 7.2 p.95

On their way to the promised land the Hebrew people are refused passage by the Edomites. What is the force of the analepsis of Num. 20.15–16?

To back up the request to pass through, the narrative takes time to recall the stay in Egypt. The narrator could have referred to the course taken through the wilderness (cf. the narrative in the book of Numbers). He prefers to evoke the foundation event of Israel (external analepsis). This important event is presented as a reminder of what Edom is thought to know – with the idea of persuading the Edomites to authorize the passage of the people of Israel through its territory. This reminder of the past allows a comparison between two oppressive peoples, Egypt and Edom. In fact, all the conditions offered by Moses' messengers (not to trample on the fields, not to depart from the way, to pay for water) come to nothing: Edom will take up arms. This episode marks the negative memory associated with the Edomites in the rest of the Bible (Amos 1.11; Ezekiel 34).

Chapter 7, 7.2 p.95

In Gen 40.12–15, Joseph interprets the dream of Pharaoh's cupbearer. Note the prolepses and analepses in these verses and specify their force.

The interpretation of the dream first of all indicates what is going to happen to the cupbearer three days later (prolepsis): Pharaoh will rehabilitate him. However, the narrative is interested in Joseph's fate. This near future becomes a present and this present is to become a moment of memory for the cupbearer. A first brief analepsis must remind him that he shared the same unfortunate condition as Joseph and prompt him to ask for his freedom from Pharaoh (v.14). The readers are reminded of the origin of Joseph's misfortunes (v.15: he was 'brought up in the country of the Hebrews', cf. Gen.37.28). This analepsis is a more major one. It makes it possible to link the story of Joseph with that of Jaocb, his father, and thus with the whole of the patriarchal history. To keep the readers in suspense, the verse ends with a third analepsis ('also I have done nothing that they should put me into the dungeon), which underlines Joseph's innocence by evoking the second betrayal of which he has been the object.

Chapter 7, 7.2 p.95

In Gen.22.8, Abraham declares to his son Isaac: 'God will provide the lamb for the sacrifice, my son.' What is the force of this prolepsis?

Abraham's sacrifice is a subtle narrative and its construction is magnificent. The reader learns from the start how the Lord orders Abraham to sacrifice his son (zero focalization). Then the narrative describes in great detail the progress of Abraham and his son towards the mountain of sacrifice (external focalization). The narrative plays on Isaac's ignorance about the victim to be sacrificed. His question forms the dramatic climax. Verse 8 anticipates the denouement of the narrative (internal prolepsis), while preserving the dramatic tension. Abraham – without knowing that the angel of the Lord will intervene – pronounces a response which by its ambiguity allows a double meaning. In the eyes of the reader the patriarch appears as a man of faith. His exemplary attitude asks to be put into practice by the readers of all centuries.

Chapter 7, 7.2 p.95

Deuteronomy 26 relates the institution of the rite of the firstfruits. Note the analepses and prolepses in the story. What is their force and their amplitude? What significance do they give to the rite?

Throughout, the narrative relates the institution of this rite in the form of a prolepsis: 'When you come into the land which the LORD your God gives you for an inheritance' (v.1). If we accept that the narrative was written during the exile, or even after the exile, this proleptic reading gives a special sense to the gift of the land. The gift of the promised land only takes on significance when it has been lost. In the words which accompany the rite, a first analepsis emphasizes the importance of this gift by its force (v.3, a reference to the promise made to the fathers); a second, by its amplitude (vv.5b-8, a resume of the whole history of the people of God from Jacob). By its interplay of prolepses and analepses, the narrative, which is more than a simple reminder of the past, leads the readers to remember their status as oppressed emigrants, freed by God; it invites them in the festival to share their land, the gift of God, with those who have no land, the levite and the emigrant.

Chapter 7, 7.3 p.100

The crossing of the Red Sea is related in Ex.13.17–14.31 and then sung in the song of Miriam and Moses (Ex.15). What effect of coupling is thus produced?

The juxtaposition of a narrative and two canticles produces effects of meaning that must not escape analysis. Note the sequence: the narrative of what has happened and then the liturgical song. The canticles of Miriam and Moses have hardly any nuances: they magnify the intervention of God and his warlike power. On the other hand, if we read the narrative of the exodus from Egypt (Ex.13.17–

14.31), it has to be acknowledged that it is not very clear how the liberation takes place: protection symbolized by the cloud (v.19), divine action through the hand of Moses, a natural phenomenon (an east wind which drives back the sea in v.21), disorder introduced into Pharaoh's camp (v.24), difficulties in the driving of the chariots (v.25)? If the conclusion is clear – God has intervened in history – the narrative allows some ambiguity in the re-reading of the event. Set side by side, these two scenes of the exodus from Egypt complement each other: the one, closer to the experience and its re-reading, seeks to discover traces of God in history; the other, more festive and liturgical, makes a joyful celebration of God break out, revealing his powerful presence in this same history.

Chapter 7, 7.3 p100

Make a careful comparison between the three accounts of the meeting between Peter and Cornelius in Acts 10.9–48; Acts 11.5–18 and Acts 15.7–11. What elements are hidden, summed up, transformed or underlined between one version and the other?

The narrative of Acts 10 has the most detail: it maintains a certain balance between the different scenes. In relationship to the facts that one finds there, Acts 11 moves on to a double arrangement. First, in his account given to the brethren in Jerusalem, Peter shows obvious caution: he conceals his first words on his arrival at Cornelius' house (10.28b) and does not say a word about his stay in Caesarea (10.48b); moreover he says specifically that he was accompanied by six witnesses (11.12b) and hides more behind the divine initiative ('Who was I to prevent God from acting?' 11.17). Secondly, Peter brings about a recentring on the action of the Spirit, by passing very rapidly over his own discourse: 'Hardly had I spoken than the Holy Spirit fell up on them. . .' (11.15); then he links this event with a declaration by the Lord (11.16). The re-reading at a distance of his encounter with the pagan world in Acts

15 makes virtually no mention of the Holy Spirit, emphasizing its ultimate consequences for believers who have come from paganism; cf. the specific details which mark the text, 'as for us', 'without making the slightest distinction between us and them', 'just as they are'.

Chapter 8, 8.1 p.106

How does the quotation from Isaiah in Mark 1.2–3 orientate the narrative of the Gospel of Mark?

Often the beginning of a narrative provides the reader with keys for its interpretation. Here the quotation is of prime importance. In narrative terms, the placing of a quotation at the beginning of the narrative allows an interesting mirror effect. Jesus, the protagonist of the Gospel, is preceded by John the Baptist, the precursor, who himself is preceded by the word of a prophet, who bears a word from God which precedes him. The story of Jesus begins in a way which is already marked by the will of the one who sends him. First of all the narrative puts Jesus in a particular relationship with God and gives a key which will make it possible to understand, as an echo, the last saying in the Gospel: 'He is going before you to Galilee; there you will see him, as he has told you' (16.7).

Chapter 8, 8.1 p.106

What point of view does the Chronicler give of the story of Saul in I Chron.10.13–14?

Verses 13–14 are visibly an explanatory gloss on the part of the narrator of the book of Chronicles. His judgment is peremptory and definitive. He remembers only Saul's bad side: faithlessness (I Sam.15), a failure to observe the word, necromancy (I Sam 28). These sins of Saul explain to the reader why God made him die and why he handed on his kingship to David. We should note that from a historical point of view the reality must have been more com-